8Up

DOWN TO EARTH

A New Vision for the Church

DOWN TO EARTH

A New Vision for the Church

Donald Reeves

MOWBRAY

Mowbray
A Cassell imprint
Wellington House, 125 Strand, London WC2R 0BB
215 Park Avenue South, New York, NY 10003

First published 1996

British Library Cataloguing-in-Publication Data
A catalogue record for this book is available from the British Library.

ISBN 0–264–67371–9

'The stranger within my gate' by Rudyard Kipling on p. 48 is quoted by permission of Macmillan Publishers Ltd.
The lines from Robert Lowell, 'Waking early Sunday morning', on p. 84 are quoted by permission of Faber and Faber.
The publishers have been unable to trace the owner of the copyright of the poem by Arthur Waskow on p. 31; if the owner contacts them, the appropriate acknowledgement will appear in any future editions.

Typeset by Keystroke, Jacaranda Lodge, Wolverhampton
Printed in Great Britain by Biddles Ltd, Guildford and King's Lynn

Contents

Acknowledgements

I would like to thank Kate Goslett, Nadir Dinshaw, Michael Bartlett, Alastair Mansfield and the Revd Mary Robbins who read the manuscript and made valuable comments. I am particularly grateful to my secretary, Linda Maude, who not only deciphered my handwriting, but encouraged me in this project. Above all, I thank the members of the community at St James's, Piccadilly, who have cheerfully put up with my preoccupation as a writer as well as my occasional absence.

Introduction

THE REASON I HAVE WRITTEN *Down to Earth* is to show how the churches can contribute modestly, positively and imaginatively to doing something about the colossal environmental and ecological problems which we have created for ourselves.

Much has been said about the survival of the planet and ways in which a more secure, sane and hopeful future might be established. Therefore I shall have little to say about these matters, although they infiltrate everything I have written.

I write from within the Christian tradition, as a priest in the Church of England, and largely out of my experience as Rector of a city-centre church, St James's, Piccadilly. *Down to Earth* is, in part, autobiography, part reflection on a city-centre ministry, but mostly a plea to the churches (or anyone else who is willing to listen) to move out of the shadows and to join those who are actively working for a safer world for their children and future generations. This is not a book about 'reforming the Church' or 'The Church of England', but the practical steps I am advocating could establish an amazing opportunity for the refounding of a dying, declining institution into a movement committed to justice and the wellbeing of the earth.

The key to *Down to Earth* is the imagination. Unless ideas and proposals for action 'catch the imagination' they will die, for the imagination shakes, disrupts and destabilizes familiar and fixed ways of understanding experience. Through symbols, metaphors, images and stories, our imagination suggests alternative and different worlds. Imagination is the crucial agent in change and transformation.[1]

After an autobiographical introduction, I propose fresh but well-tried ways of knowing or imagining God (Chapter 2). I hint at what a society could be like where the notion of the 'public' is celebrated. Strangers are welcomed, and the struggle against racism, so endemic in Britain, is sustained (Chapter 3). I suggest ways in which the cherishing of the inner life will transform the practice of leadership (Chapters 4 and 5). Ritual is shown to be a neglected way in which we can help one another to manage change (Chapter 6). In Chapter 7 I trace my relationship to the Bible – and through the writing of a particular sermon indicate what it is like to imagine the world through the biblical text 'as if' we have come from God, and are dependent on God and are moving into the consummation of everything in God. In Chapter 8 I explore the implications of men disengaging themselves from the patriarchal structures which they created and under which we all live. And in Chapter 9 I sketch the outlines of alternative Christian-based ecological communities.

Because this is a book for the future, I have dedicated it to three members of the community at St James's, Piccadilly – Rachel Mabey, Benjamin Nakama, and Charles Coe. Their average age is 16 months.

NOTE

1 Walter Brueggemann has been an inspiration to me in discovering the imagination as the source of change – particularly in *The Prophetic Imagination* (London: SCM Press, 1978), *Hopeful Imagination – Prophetic Voices in Exile* (Philadelphia: Fortress Press, 1986), *Finally Comes the Poet* (Philadelphia: Fortress Press, 1989), and *The Bible and Post Modern Imagination* (London: SCM Press, 1993).

1

From Chichester to Piccadilly

IN NOVEMBER 1980 I came to St James's church, Piccadilly, as its new Rector. The then Bishop of London, Gerald Ellison, told me: 'I don't care what you do, but keep the church open. You have a big job.'

The Bishop's comments about a big job was an understatement. I soon discovered that there was only a handful of people associated with the church, and they drifted away in my first few weeks. And there were no funds. We were bankrupt.

But I inherited something less tangible, and more difficult to handle than the lack of people or money, and that was the reputation of St James's, Piccadilly. It represented, at least in popular imagination, the quintessential character of the Church of England – restrained, moderate, wealthy and privileged. The person of the Rector was someone to be reckoned with. Among my 21 predecessors there are five archbishops, two bishops, three deans, three archdeacons and numerous prebendaries and canons. The church 'for the rich' it was called – though no one would guess from the collections – and for fashionable weddings and memorial services with 'good music'. And that was all.

I had just completed thirteen years as Vicar of St Peter's church on the St Helier estate in Morden, one of the largest parishes in South London. There my vicarage was a modest, functional 1930s house tucked away behind the 1930s church, and next to the church hall. In 1980 I moved into St James's Rectory. It is the only private house in Piccadilly. It had an air of faded grandeur with a staircase leading up to the front door, flanked by a flourish of railings. Over the entrance are the words '*Ad dei gloriam,*

salutem populi, post belli incendia, Refectae surrexerunt Aeds. AD MCMLVI.
Nisi Dominus Aedif. For some days I felt uncomfortable coming in and
out of this pretentious entrance, and used the back door instead.

I had no blueprint and no strategy. City-centre churches are the
Cinderellas of the Church of England; they have limited functions. There
were no models which were available to me – no experience on which
I could draw. But I had some intuition about various possibilities. Some
of these intuitions were little more than hunches which were disastrous in
their outcome; some were inspired guesswork. But others provoked my
imagination in such a way that they broke away from familiar and well-tried
paths into surprising and new directions. Blake's dictum that everything
begins with the imagination has been absolutely true of my best work; I was
pleased to discover that he was baptized at St James's, Piccadilly, and lived
for a time in the parish – in Golden Square.[1]

Intuitions have their roots; those which have been significant were
formed way back in my childhood.

I was the only child of middle-class parents. My father owned a garage
in Chichester, and after it was bombed during the war he joined the Navy.
He was away from the time I was six. By the time he returned I hardly
knew him – a state of affairs which lasted until his death. My mother was
an attractive, energetic woman. Nothing pleased her more to be thought
of as my sister when I was in my early twenties.

But parenting did not come easily to my mother and father: just after
their marriage they acquired a short-haired terrier; a photograph shows their
delight. Next to it is another photograph of my father awkwardly holding
a baby – me – and my mother looking on perplexed and apprehensive.

Neither of my parents was interested in religion. My mother had an eye
for handsome clergymen; she enjoyed flirting with them when she came
across them. But they both felt religion and church was not for them.
Religion was never discussed. I was, of course, christened, but only just.
My mother arranged a party before the service; I was told they arrived late
at the church and realized that I had been forgotten, so the service was
delayed while I was collected. Years later, when I announced that I was
going to be ordained, my parents were surprised and disappointed. They
felt I should do a proper job. They felt there was something illegitimate
about the clergy. They believed the clergy were perpetuating a sham and
a delusion. Their vehemence was upsetting, since it was so unexpected.

My most intense memories of religion as a boy were associated with
Chichester Cathedral. My mother often used the Cathedral as a short
cut from one street to another; and it was there, on one of her shopping
expeditions, when I was about nine, that I met Arthur Duncan-Jones, the

Dean of Chichester. He promptly invited me to visit him at the Deanery. He seemed to me to be the oldest man in the world. I would visit him in his library-cum-study. I sat on the library ladder; the Dean, in black apron and gaiters (which bishops and deans then wore), sat at his desk. And we talked – a bit about my school, which I hated. Never about my parents, about whom I was beginning to be ashamed. Never about religion. It was the first time in my life that anyone, particularly such a formidable man as the Dean, had taken a real interest in me. He treated this grave little boy with immense seriousness and respect. He already had an extensive family of his own, but I felt 'adopted', and the Deanery, on my occasional visits, became a second home.

At 5 o'clock the Dean's Verger came to escort the Dean to the Cathedral for Evensong. Astonished, I watched the Dean dress himself in a series of curious garments – cassock, a long-sleeved surplice, tippet, preaching scarf and bands; and when all was complete he placed a black skullcap on his head. Holding my hand, we would process to the Cathedral.

I came to love Chichester Cathedral. I felt completely safe there – at home in its shadows, secure in the nave and under its arches which enfolded me. I can still recall the acrid smell of the coal-burning stoves which heated the Cathedral, and by which in winter I warmed myself. Although my parents did their very best for me, yet I was never truly at home in my home, so the Cathedral became that home. As soon as I could on my return to Chichester for the holidays I would go to the Cathedral.

Slowly over a period I came to appreciate the liturgy – particularly the music. The organist, Dr Hawkins, had been taught by the French composer and organist Charles Widor. 'Hawky', as he was called, improvised like Widor, and on festival days there was High Mass – with clouds of incense, massed trumpets and magnificent vestments. I understood very little of the liturgy; I was like a spectator at some entrancing theatrical event. I did not kneel – if I did I disappeared behind the stall in the choir, so I sat, my legs dangling, and watched as my friend, the Dean, celebrated the Eucharist.

But there was one aspect of the liturgy which intrigued me. I told no one, but I noticed it every time. I had gathered that the most solemn movement of the service was when the people left their seats and knelt at the altar rail to receive Communion. I noticed as they returned, one by one, how thoughtful, gentle and sometimes sad their faces had become. Most of the Cathedral congregation seemed to me to be almost as old as the Dean: I was scared of them all, and whenever I was with the Dean, and they wanted to talk to him, I would move behind him, hoping not to be noticed. But the transformation of these men and women, usually so ferocious, into something quite vulnerable was, and remains to this day, a mystery.

Although I have celebrated the Eucharist countless times over thirty years, the mystery of those changed faces is with me still. I, too, have occasionally had a sense of this mystery: the first time I celebrated the Holy Communion at All Saints church, Maidstone, where I was a curate, was at 8 o'clock on a Sunday morning with a tiny congregation. Facing the high altar as I leant over the chalice and paten, I caught my face as in a mirror, reflected on the over-polished, slightly scratched paten on which the wafers lay. I saw myself as I said the words 'This is my body . . . this is my blood, given for you'.

I visited Arthur Duncan-Jones a few days before he died. He was sitting up in bed with a shawl over his shoulders, and his black skullcap was askew. He was chewing a chicken bone. His eyes lit up as I came into the room; he was always so pleased to see me. But he was at his most irascible, because he was going to miss one of the highlights of the Cathedral year – the Epiphany Carol Service.

After his death my love affair with the Cathedral ended. Anyhow, I came less to Chichester. I later knew Walter Hussey, the next Dean. I admired his passion for the arts, but it was not the same. I found the liturgy trivial and lifeless, and the preaching dull and uninspired.

My reason for writing about Chichester is simply that my connections with Christianity and the Church were minimal at Sherborne School, then during National Service and as a student at Queens' College, Cambridge, where I read English. Certainly, I was confirmed at Sherborne, as were the rest of my contemporaries. My confirmation was entirely unmemorable, except for the presence of a large number of flies in the chapel. The bishop who was confirming was a big man. He had a florid complexion. When he was not speaking he would leave his mouth open. I spent the whole service staring at him, wondering if he would swallow a fly. As an adolescent I was concerned to survive Sherborne – coping with bullying, trying to avoid being noticed, enjoying all sorts of sexual experiments; above all, surviving the onslaught to have 'House spirit' focused on the worship of everything athletic. With these hefty pressures, religion, understandably, hardly featured.

At Cambridge, apart from the occasional visit to Great St Mary's, the University Church where Mervyn Stockwood (whose chaplain I was later to become) was Vicar, and Little St Mary's, the nearest I could find to Chichester Cathedral, I was not interested in religion.

Only once was I seriously bothered. Billy Graham held a mission. Out of curiosity I went. When the time came for those who wanted to take matters further were invited to stand up, I did so. Some days later one of Billy Graham's team came to see me. He threatened and cajoled me into taking Christ as my Lord and Saviour. I was not used to talking about God and sin and the need for repentance: for a lot of the time I did not understand what he was talking about. During much of this conversation, he brandished a large Bible, quoting texts at me. As a result it was many years before I could properly appreciate the Bible; I developed a strong aversion to it. After three hours I gave in; I knelt with him against my old sofa of cracked and polished leather, and received Jesus Christ. I was relieved when he left; but I could not bring myself to read the tracts he left with me.

Some days later I received a letter from him. He told me that on his way back to Oxford, he prayed aloud on the bus with joy that I was now saved. 'Another scalp', I thought. I wanted to have nothing more to do with Christianity. That abuse has remained with me ever since. Over the years at St James's, Piccadilly, a steady number of people from the major London Evangelical churches like Holy Trinity, Brompton, have found their way to St James's, Piccadilly, and after much debriefing some have found their home with us. Evangelicals are the most vociferous in their attacks on the cults; little do they realize how they mirror the things they attack in others.

In 1957 I left Cambridge and went to Beirut to work as lecturer for the British Council. Beirut was then at the edge of its descent into hell; but for a young, untried Englishman it was the best of all cosmopolitan cities. My job was not arduous. I had time and energy to join in a hectic social life; an unattached Englishman was both a curiosity and in demand.

But I began to feel steadily isolated. And I realized that whatever else I was to do it was not to have a career in the British Council. I enjoyed teaching English and arranging cultural events, but I was restless, a little homesick; letters from my Cambridge friends were what I looked forward to. My personal life began to resemble an Italian opera; I found myself in emotional situations over which I had no control. I had no friend, no one whom I trusted to talk with. After a particularly difficult experience, where I had been physically in great danger, I started each day by sitting in a garish, modern, Franciscan Catholic church in Rue Hamra. I sat there for twenty minutes or so – being as quiet in my self as I could. After some months my life became easier; everything eased.

I continued going to the church. I just sat, and tried to be quiet. No one spoke to me: I always sat at the back. People came in and out during the weekday Masses. Sometimes, after a late night, it was difficult to get up for my daily visit. More often when I was there I wondered what I was doing. But for some months I went – sat and tried to be still.

I went to rid myself of guilt, confusion of every sort, and a restlessness about my entire life; I was desperate to do something about the obsessive side of my nature which caused havoc among so many people. So I sat. Over those months, I began, fleetingly, to have a sense that my experiences of self-loathing were not, and need not be, paramount. Instead, occasionally I began to know that I was accepted, prized; this experience was like receiving a special gift. It was not mediated through friendship, or a love affair, or another person; it was a conviction which grew within me. I can only describe this experience as religious; I had never searched for God, looked for God or even thought much about God. I knew next to nothing about Jesus Christ; except for those early days in the Cathedral, and a brief relationship with an Anglo-Catholic church (p. 17 below), church services were just a blur in my memory – something to be endured. But there in Beirut, troubled and isolated as I was, God had searched me out, and touched me.

A biochemist or psychotherapist could rapidly explain away all this – just a case of hormonal imbalance or an identity crisis, but these explanations do not do justice to the experience. For as a result of my visit to that church, and coming to terms with myself, my life changed. It was not just that I became calmer, but also I began to experience a call, a summons to live a more useful life, to be less self-concerned, and to be more generous. This was not just an idea which came out of the blue, it was a call. The 'passive' voice is more pertinent than the 'active' voice. The call was to become a priest.

I recognize the oddness of this experience. We are now accustomed to seeing ourselves as independent, autonomous persons, reduced to considering ourselves as customers or consumers. That we are addressed by one who is not us, who is an inscrutable mystery which cannot be seduced, captured or possessed, is strange indeed.

This decision to become a priest disturbed, frightened and surprised me. I knew nothing about the Church of England. I began to attend the little Anglican church, St George's, in Beirut. There was Matins – the women wore hats, and the men their Sunday suits. There was choir practice and coffee mornings, harvest festivals and carol services. On special days, the Ambassador would read the second lesson.

I began to prove myself; I created courses in Christian masochism. I read St Mark's Gospel, and was thrown by its radical demands; I started to read the Bible every day with notes provided by the Bible Reading Fellowship. They were excessively pious. I abandoned the Bible shortly afterwards, and started a hectic life of prayer. Forgetting the hours spent in church, just being still, I produced lists of people and things to pray for – morning and evening. I prayed for myself that I would be worthy to answer this summons. I tried to do without drink, without sex – I was determined to keep my emotions in control. The more I prayed the worse it became, because I was in a no-win situation: trying to be a spiritual Rambo, fighting the good fight. But the battle was lost, before it began.

The harder I tried to be good, because this is what I told myself I must be, the more I failed, and the more wretched I became. And if by any chance I succeeded for a while, then I realized I was guilty of the cardinal sin – pride; I had to start all over again. The knowledge of being prized and valued was lost amongst this cheerless, spiritual shambles.

My life, outwardly, carried on as before. No one guessed how I was. I was scared of being ridiculed if I announced my intention of being ordained. On leave in England, the Bishop of Chichester arranged for me to attend a selection conference – run, then, much on the lines of the War Office Selection Board organized for recruiting National Service Officers. I passed. I went to visit a theological college – a bleak Gothic building on the edge of a field. The principal was most lugubrious. The students told me that he lived on onion soup, and that his favourite topic for sermons was death. I was offered a place but left as quickly as I could; 'If that was Christianity, then give me measles', I said to myself.

I returned to Beirut. Putting the idea of ordination out of mind, I tried to resume my feverish spiritual exercises, but abandoned most of them.

Eventually, I went to Cuddesdon Theological College. I had resigned from the British Council, after being posted back to London to take a course in the teaching of English as a foreign language. In Beirut, I had come across a radical church magazine, *Prism*; I got to know Christopher Martin, its editor. Through him I was invited to be Director of Studies at Brasted – a pre-theological college for non-graduates. There I enjoyed teaching a wide range of courses on elementary philosophy, English literature and church history. While at Brasted I decided to go ahead with ordination. I was accepted as a student at Cuddesdon, where Robert Runcie was principal.

My time at Cuddesdon was important, not because I learnt much theology, but because through the disciplined life of prayer and study, I began to get a sense of the Church in which I was to work. Here was a framework into which I could fit; but I never fitted easily. I found the compulsory silences irksome, and they were usually ignored. I enjoyed being organist of the spectacular village church in Cuddesdon: I wrote a rumbustious Nativity play which upset most of the college, and some of the village.

In the 1960s there were plenty of jobs available anywhere in England. Ordinands could be, and were, particular as to where they served their curacies. I did not mind where I went. When I was sent to All Saints church, Maidstone, for an introductory weekend, I was glad to go. Neil Nye, the Vicar, and I liked each other. After a busy Saturday afternoon constructing angels' wings for the Christmas play, and a long conversation, I accepted his invitation. I was ordained deacon in June 1963, and a year later the Archbishop of Canterbury, Michael Ramsay, ordained me priest in Canterbury Cathedral.

Sixteen years later I moved to Piccadilly. My previous job had not prepared me for this move. I inherited an empty, English baroque church in the centre of London. I had to start all over again; the memories of those early experiences I have described were formative in establishing St James's.

*   *   *

There are several aspects of this remembering which are pertinent. One is that I have always tried to honour all human experience. One of the curses of organized religion is the split between mind and body, reason and emotion. This dualism creates all that is reactionary in religion. A separate spiritual realm is invented and surrounded with a variety of practices invariably designed to appease a stern, remote and uncompromising god – and leaving the world much as it is. But I have learnt personally and from others that God's grace and goodness is mediated through the mess and muddle of our existence, and not just through the narrow channels of the church.

This was brought home to me when I was domestic chaplain to Mervyn Stockwood, the Bishop of Southwark. After six months in the job, I realized I had lost my faith and ceased to believe in God. The excitement leading up to my ordination continued as a curate. Then it began to evaporate. I just lost interest in God; this indifference gave way to a numbness about God, which eventually changed into anger about the stupidity of so much organized religion.

My job was demanding. Much of it I did not enjoy. I may have been depressed, but depression only describes the condition; and depression was not entirely accurate since I managed to function fairly well in other parts of my life. I have since recognized that this condition is almost an inevitable part of life. Those dark periods, where even the desire to know God vanishes, can be times of growth, as well as times of testing. The mystical tradition describes these experiences as the dark night of the soul. That may be so, but that is a rather too exalted description for what is, after all, confusing and debilitating. A period of intense counselling helped me out of this mess, and on leaving the Bishop of Southwark, and before I went to work in south London, I attended a training course at the Urban Training Centre in Chicago, where both faith and hope were surprisingly renewed.

I mention what I believe is a fairly commonplace experience, because in 1980 I wanted to draw together a Christian community which would be as inclusive as possible and where the boundaries would be blurred; it would be a church where anyone would be invited to feel at home – pioneers, explorers, the radical and disaffected, as well as the confused, conservative and cautious; I could hardly do less given my own chequered experience.

The image of the journey is one of the most popular ways to describe the Christian life. The pilgrim is an amalgam of images – a tall, gaunt individual, weather-hardened, rugged. I see him on top of a ridge, resting on a wooden staff, looking out across the land. I am reminded of Charlton Heston, a woodcut from Bunyan's *Pilgrim's Progress*, and St Francis of Assisi. He knows where he is going and how he is going to get there. His clarity is enviable because the spiritual journey is rarely like that. (Moreover, the solitary maleness of the image reduces its power.) For me the journey is more often a slouch, or an amble; occasionally the walker sprints a short distance. At best it is a gentle, unhurried walk in the company of friends where the journey is as important as the destination. Sometimes, and for long periods, the traveller stops, lies under a rock letting the world go by.

Since the churches are losing numbers, the drive for membership has become a significant feature. I know that working out a Christian vocation is tough and rigorous, but the journey in which everyone is travelling (even though they may not recognize it or feel easy with the image) is not just for those who conform easily or thoughtlessly to conventional religion; all are welcome.

Therefore it was inevitable that I wanted the church to be a welcoming, receiving place, offering hospitality, where, as it were, the guest's experience was attended to as much as the host's so that sometimes it becomes difficult to distinguish the two. Cities need places where people can meet, rest, feel safe, be quiet, celebrate, meet strangers and be at home. Most churches are now kept securely locked, as if they were only of interest to thieves.

I was not immediately at home in Piccadilly. It was not just the rectory, but also the church. Thus, the night before the Bishop instituted me to the 'living', I locked myself in the building. I was not going to let the building or the job defeat me. I had to own the building; I was not going to be overawed by the impeccable, chaste, slightly extravagant restoration of Christopher Wren's work by Sir Albert Richardson. I lay prostrate on the floor. I knelt and I crouched. I walked and ran up and down and round the aisles. I sat on the altar. I ranted from the pulpit. I hummed and I sang. I hugged the pillars. I cursed God, and praised God. I prayed for strength, for passion and for luck. I knew I was going to need it. I was not going to be defeated by anyone, and God had to know how I felt. The next day I was formally installed, in the presence of many dignitaries and friends. I rang the bell. Meekly, I followed the Archdeacon as he led me to the font, the lectern, the pulpit and the altar. No one knew that I had already arrived.

Realizing how intimidating church buildings can be, particularly for those whose memories of church are not happy ones, I created a ritual in the early 1980s for those who used the church for vigils, protests, celebrations or demonstrations. I discovered two seventeenth-century beadle staves. The beadles used them when they were distributing alms to the poor of the parish. Knowing how beadles were regarded by the poor, I suspect that the staves were also used to keep them at bay, when the aristocrats arrived at St James's for morning prayer. As part of my welcome, I symbolically broke one stave in half, as a way of breaking the monopoly of the wealthy, and inviting everyone to feel at home.

Whether it was the way I came to be a Christian, or whether it happened as a result, my natural, timid and conservative nature has altered over the years. I have found being a Christian a considerable nuisance. I have rarely experienced the desire and the longing to love God, which is one of the hallmarks of the saint and mystic. Instead, I have, as it were, been taken by the scruff of the neck and told to get on with it. I have often wished for a quieter life, but it has eluded me. I have sometimes felt like Teresa of Avila, who nearly drowned in a flood. She exclaimed to God 'If this is how you treat your friends, no wonder you have so few of them'.

I have therefore grown up as a Christian to test belief against experience, not just personal experience, but against all the turbulence of the world. In the 1980s, I opposed the Falkland Islands venture, and said so. I found the arguments for the Campaign for Nuclear Disarmament increasingly attractive. But I became aware of the vacuum in our public and political life. There had to be some coherent, alternative vision to that of the market place. During the 1980s St James's became one of a number of public forums where these preoccupations could be discussed – notably through the Dunamis Project.[2]

What I noticed, and living in central London it could not be otherwise, was the victims of the policies of the Conservative Party. I mean the growing underclass in Britain, disaffected young people, the homeless and mentally ill – among them those who wander in our streets; those caught in the 'poverty trap', the long-term unemployed, the forgotten rural and mining communities decimated by the relentless pressures of the Market where everything has a price tag.

Yet the victims of change are nearly all of us – so ubiquitous are the pressures of the Market. In the early 1970s, as a young south London vicar, I went to meetings of the local Tenants Association and Labour Party. There were always one or two Marxists at these meetings. Every dispute with the then Tory Greater London Council or local Council found its place in the Marxist scheme of things. I was amazed at how the smallest dispute, about refuse collection or the maintenance of tenants' houses, could be readily related to the class struggle and the Cold War, and everything else!

Now the 'class struggle' has been replaced by the Market, which is more than pure economics; it has become a broad principle of life. I know farmers, lawyers, publishers, civil servants, media executives, social workers, university teachers, doctors and nurses – just about every professional person who in the last ten years have had to change their behaviour, their conduct at work. At heart they may still be good social democrats, but now they have learnt to become aggressive managers, accountants and entrepreneurs. Their mission statements and appraisal forms, their cost benefit analyses – this is now what matters. We are all customers and consumers who mimic the Market. That is the Thatcherite project which has changed the face of our institutions and the people who run them.

The human cost of this project is rarely noticed; at least in former days there were divisions between work and the rest of life. Now there is, at least for the young professional, only work – flexitime it is called. You should be there half an hour before you wake up, and you should be leaving an hour after you leave.

I have seen what the Thatcherite project has done to people – to relationships, to families and to children. One Good Friday I noticed a well-dressed man in his early thirties walking distractedly round the garden at St James's, Piccadilly. He was an advertising executive working nearby. His office was open as usual even though it was Good Friday. But he had had enough. Ten years he had given to his job. Now his marriage had finished; he was a stranger to his children. So he resigned. He could take no more. As he finished talking to me, he looked at me directly, and through his tears said 'And the Church doesn't help; you have nothing to say to me'.

He is absolutely right. As spectators of change or victims of it, there seems to be no alternative on offer, not even the possibility of new horizons, new steps to be taken. I could offer a listening ear as I did to that young man – but that was all I could do.

That man's accusation has stayed with me ever since. There has to be a future, which is not just a repetition of the present. Where should I look for those seeking alternatives? Not to our traditional organizations; political parties, trades unions, the churches, all are in decline. There is general disaffection with politics. It seemed briefly, towards the end of the 1980s, that a new agenda of issues, previously unrecognized, began to coincide with considerable public anxieties – these issues gathered under the umbrella of the environment. Questions about climatic changes, or endangered species, or transport, or intensive agriculture, were gradually becoming part of the consciousness of parliament, government and industry.

But with the collapse of the Berlin Wall everything has changed. The tension between capitalism and communism has disappeared overnight, and confidence that government is willing or capable of addressing massive and complex environmental problems has evaporated.

Yet alongside this crisis of confidence with traditional institutions, there are other changes of a more positive kind. Robin Grove-White, Director of the Centre for the Study of Environmental Change, Lancaster University, in a speech given at the Annual Meeting of the Green Alliance at the Royal Society of Arts in November 1994 put it like this:

> There is a growing proliferation of new, frequently fragile, but vibrant social networks developing around practices concerned with such issues as health, food, gender, personal growth and spiritual development, counselling, leisure, animals, co-ops of all kinds, new religious networks in the cities.[3]

It may be, as he goes on to say, 'These concatenations of these cultural kinds should be regarded as species of narcissism or escapism or as matters of simple private concerns'. Or they may be 'harbingers of how new forms of collective action, of collective interdependence appropriate to modern, culturally diverse sustainable societies are going to emerge and crystallise'.[4]

It is too early to make an accurate judgement about this fledgling cultural movement, but what is undeniable, at the heart of such fragile and bewildering diversity, is a moral impulse, a moral resonance and a refusal to be co-opted into apathy and fatalism. Many persons involved in these networks have been and are associated with St James's, Piccadilly, and the moral concern with which so many of these activities are undertaken is palpable.

The churches have a modest part to play in this burgeoning. I interpret these more positive movements as a sign of God luring us into life. A church which is blind or deaf to God, either unwillingly or deliberately, is guilty of apostasy: turning away from God in the pursuit of other gods. To call any church apostate is serious, and it is certainly a generalization which can be contradicted in the lives of many individuals, but I do not know how else to describe the weariness, the exhaustion of spirit, which I have observed sometimes in myself and others. Has the dinosaur of religious institutions sucked and squashed the life out of us?

The Church of England is my constituency. I have come to love it, but also to be infuriated by it. Yet I would not find myself at home in any other church. We are so engrossed with ourselves, our survival, our future, that it frequently looks as if we believe there is no life beyond our walls. Therefore, as we are, we are not able to excite people's imaginations, evoke much sense of idealism, or contribute to the process of 'waking up' to the opportunities for creating a different common future. Moreover, the church has made so many concessions to the existing culture, colluded with the fantasies of consumer paradise for all, that we have almost forfeited our right to participate.

Modesty should be the key to whatever contribution Christianity can make, because it is absurd to propose that 'religion has all the answers'. Religion cannot answer every question. But what I do know is that at its best the Christian faith communicates a story which provides meaning and makes sense in the face of guilt, wickedness, suffering and death, and of grace, joy and hope. I have experienced how true Christianity empowers women and men, and guarantees and celebrates our highest ideals. I know how true Christianity provides a steady, consistent basis of love and trust which are nourished by allegiance to a particular community; and how the language of Christian belief does justice (in a way so much trivialized and reduced language does not) to our longings and desires for all that is good, and of God. I have seen how true Christianity has provided a base for protest and resistance against injustice – as in our own day among those for whom liberation has rightly been their abiding passion.

I know how these claims so directly and baldly stated are easily contradicted by other experiences. Indictments of organized religion are formidable and do not need to be repeated.

As we are, we can only be among the silent bystanders. But having said that, and anything else that can be said, perhaps too easily, about 'The Church', I know it is possible to move out of the shadows and to take our part willingly, modestly and in humility. *Down to Earth* proposes some markers for us all to follow, and there is no more important subject to begin with than with 'God'.

NOTES

1 To honour William Blake, I was one among others who founded the William Blake Society in 1984, whose object is to honour his prophetic genius.

2 The Dunamis Project was founded in 1980 to explore issues of personal, national and international security. It has created a successful public forum for the exploration of alternative approaches to the pursuit of international security, for examining the psychological, moral and spiritual links between personal security and the security of nations, and for holding up a vision of a stable and just world.

3 Robin Grove-White, *Environment and Society: Some Reflections* (The Green Alliance, 49 Wellington Street, London WC2E 7BN), p. 6.

4 *Environment and Society*, p. 8.

CHAPTER

2

Where on earth
is God?

Who has not found the heaven below
will fail of it above
For angels rent the house next door
wherever we remove.
Emily Dickinson[1]

ON 20 JULY 1969, Neil Armstrong landed on the moon; as he touched its surface, he said 'One small step for a man, one giant leap for mankind!' This mission was greeted with almost universal euphoria. Then there seemed to be no limits to our aspirations and ambitions. To conquer space meant we could conquer anything.

Christianity affirms that humanity is made 'in the image of God', but the moon landing celebrated not just the start of mastery of the planet, but potentially of the universe as we began to peep into distant galaxies. We had become like gods.

The journey to the moon was the final triumph of belief in progress: the last manifestation of the 'culture' of the Enlightenment; by culture I mean the usually unspoken assumptions or understandings of the way things are.[2] These included the certainty that man was the measure of all things, that reason was supreme, and that the scientific method of analysis and experiment was the only way to truth. Reality was 'before' us – to be manipulated, examined, ordered and analysed. This was simply and directly expressed by Alexander Pope:

Nature and Nature's laws lay hid in night:
God said, *Let Newton be!* and all was light.

The space project, for all its hubris and persistent over-estimating of our capacities, fits oddly into the twentieth century because confidence in progress, reason and the goal of life as human happiness had evaporated long ago. It is not difficult to see why this was so. Trust in the whole human project was shattered by the dropping of the atomic bomb on Hiroshima and Nagasaki, since it dawned on us that at the touch of a button the planet's fate was in our hands. Our century has also witnessed major acts of genocide: the Turkish massacre of the Armenians, the mass murder in Stalin's camps, the killing fields of Cambodia, the genocide of our own day; and most chilling of all, the meticulous planning of the death of six million Jews destroyed once and for all the modern belief in human greatness. Hans Küng, in his classic study of Judaism, quotes Eugene Borowitz:

We believed in the goodness of man, and trusted that education and culture would direct it rightly, while psychotherapy healed its rifts. We counted on politics to bring in the Messiah, with assistance from social science. We followed the commandments of self-realisation, and looked forward to perfecting humankind. Sitting in our homes, walking on the way, lying down, rising up, we spoke of human progress and put our faith in new projects. For us, humanity sat on God's throne.[3]

There are also other movements which have challenged the Western, colonizing, white, male power base of Enlightenment thinking: Islam, liberation movements, the women's movement and the green movement.

The dismantling of the Enlightenment culture (which is still going on around us) has plunged the world into a time of confusion, anxiety and danger. With so many competing voices to be heard, and so little agreement as to common values, it is not difficult to recognize how precarious even the most experienced of democracies have become.

Christianity has also experienced a loss of confidence. We can no longer voice grand truths which are universally understood and agreed, let alone heeded. God as 'sovereign' is questioned in the face of the immensity of the suffering and evil in the world. Christian teaching and the study of the Bible have been eroded by sharp analysis and dissection of texts. But the most significant and most concrete evidence of our confusion is that which reaches down into every living room – questions about morality and personal behaviour and the limits of medical technology. Surveys have shown a scepticism about public institutions (which lay claim to tell people how to behave), and at the same time much moral concern, with a high value placed on individual autonomy.[4]

Since we have turned ourselves into gods, God has been banished. If God is anywhere then God is so remote as not to matter or has become so shrunken, so private, so personal as to make no difference.

Certainly, learning about the environmental crisis has made me realize that we are on our own. This planet is our home. There is nowhere else to go. There is no deliverer who will come and make everything new after the apocalypse.

I was brought up to believe that there was some fundamental order to creation, that the seasons would follow naturally one after another and that 'the whole world was in His hands'. Yet this is not so: the whole world is in our hands. I find this a frightening prospect. One of the things that is a great comfort to me has been that those who will live in my home on the edge of the Cotswolds when I am dead will enjoy the same landscape as I do now. I hope that the round hills, the clumps of trees on the sky-lines – remnants of one of the famous forests of England, the Wychwood Forest, the Evenlode river – often in full flood, and the hedgerows, the home of so much busy wild life, will always be there for others to enjoy. I have made a minute contribution for that future in planting trees and bushes in my garden which I will never see fully grown. But now I know that I cannot take that landscape for granted; the cycle of seasons cannot even be guaranteed. Meanwhile, hedgerows are cut down, trees disappear; there is not such a variety of birds. As I write, no cuckoos have been heard this year, the swallows are late in coming, and the last owls to have been heard at night were eight years ago.

To know that this could be so is to experience the world as that of an orphan. It is to feel quite alone. There is no God who will send us rain, or fair weather, or intervene to save us. We are on our own. God, or at least the God that I am hinting at, has disappeared: God no longer exists.

But what about the revelation of God through the Church – in worship, in the sacraments, through preaching and teaching? Has God disappeared there as well?

The best way to answer this question is to describe my own experience as a young man, when I belonged to an Anglo-Catholic parish church for a time after leaving Chichester Cathedral.

The church building, 1930s, red brick; inside I can still recall the smell of incense, flowers and floor polish on the floor. There were screens and iron grilles dividing the sanctuary from the congregation; behind the screens, there was a long altar; in the centre a tabernacle, where the sacrament was reserved. Above it, a candle flickered denoting the Real Presence. The altar was a place of mystery, power and authority. No one passed by it without genuflecting. Except for the women who arranged the flowers, no woman went into the sanctuary. The vestry was the other area which was out of bounds. Once I looked in when it was empty – a large room with rows of locked cupboards where the church silver was stored, and the vestments kept. The priests were called Father, and always wore cassocks. The Vicar was inordinately shy, a grave man with warm blue eyes.

The most important time of the week was the High Mass on Sunday, where a long and complex ritual would take place. As a young organist I used to play for this service, once I had learned how to improvise, and how to accompany plainsong. The congregation was mostly women and some young families; it was a relaxed and cheerful fellowship. The sermons were short, pithy, and declamatory – declaring what it was that the Church taught and we were to believe. Here was a church, confident in doctrine, sure that its teaching, handed down from Jesus Christ to his apostles, to the bishops and to the clergy, was safeguarded – the truth revealed in Christ. The authority of the Church was not questioned.

Our lives centred on the High Mass each Sunday morning but there were also weekday services we were encouraged to attend, retreats for the very holy, and confessions to prepare for. It was an all-consuming life with social gatherings, choir outings, gossip about Father X or Y, fasting during Lent, and no meat on Fridays.

Looking back (in fact what made me leave) was that I soon discovered everyday life was not valued. Church mattered above everything else. The rest of life was secondary. The Church provided security, certainty, and for those who sought it, comfort and consolation.

What happens when anyone moves beyond the church walls is put graphically in an educational context in the novel *Petals of Blood* by Ngugi Wa Thiongo'o. Godfrey Murissa is a teacher in a village school:

> One day, Godfrey Murissa takes his pupils out into the open air away from the four walls of their classroom. The subject matter is botany, and Murissa's purpose is to provide the learners with fingertips-on vivid experience. He teaches the children the names of the flowers and the names of their constituent parts . . . But the fragile social order between himself and the children begins to crumble when the children happen on vivid poetic metaphors to describe flowers, for example they see a red bean flower as having petals of blood, thus giving the very novel its title, and when noticing that some of the flowers are worm-eaten, they ask disquieting questions about why in this world beauty gets destroyed. The

children are not satisfied with this answer and press him further with formidable questions about humankind, about law, about God, about nature ... 'Murissa swore he would never again take the children to the fields.' He preferred the security – as Ngugi poignantly puts it, of 'dispensing knowledge to a concentration of faces looking up'.[5]

That is the strong voice of conservative religion: the knowledge, and the power which accompanies it, resides in the priest; everyone else, above all the women who make up most of the congregation, is required to be silent and passive. Their experience, memories and stories, their dreads, sufferings, dreams and hopes, their attitudes to life, to the world, to others, to their work – none of this is trusted, valued or welcomed.

Today, faith in God begins with our reflection on experience, not in some vague notion that 'God won't let it happen' or among the cynical that 'it may be God's will' that the future will collapse, and life on earth may cease. But it is difficult to discover just what we know and what we feel; it is difficult to trust our experience since we are encouraged to ignore it, deny it and not to be aware of it; thus so many remain immobilized and paralysed, settling for comfort.

There are at least four ways to describe what prevents us from trusting our experience and learning from it. The first is addiction. Environmentalists often describe how we have become entranced with our present way of life with its vision of a consumer paradise, and 'shop till you drop' (at least for those who can afford it). It is no use telling addicts to change their ways; they know their situation, but they cannot stop. That is the nature of addiction. Once the addict discovers that she has a deep desire to change, shares this desire with others, and comes to terms with her own self-disgust, she begins to perceive she can live for a greater good, and contribute to it. The Twelve Steps is the process by which addicts can be slowly released from their addiction. Alcoholics Anonymous, and similar peer groups working without the benefit of experts, are one of the most liberating and positive ways of dealing with addiction.

Denial is another way in which reality is consciously or unconsciously repudiated. Denial serves as a natural defence mechanism to protect us from excessive anxiety; it is one of the ways in which anxiety is controlled and reduced. It is an easy step to withdraw from a recognition of a difficult problem, to deny the gravity of it, and then that it exists at all; and given all the distractions of 'business as usual', denial has plenty of opportunities to flourish. Certainly I have experienced in learning about the environment such a dissonance between the 'business as usual' world and the reality of what is coming, that it is easy to wonder not whether the world has gone mad, but whether I am going that way and therefore it would be more convenient to ignore it!

Denial involves splitting off – particularly those dark, violent and aggressive aspects of our personalities. This aspect of denial has been well explored by the psychiatrist, Robert Lifton, in his writing on the psychological effects of nuclear weapons. Because we are not able to integrate the alarming possibility of eliminating all human life – with all the attendant guilt, powerlessness and paranoia, ever since Hiroshima – Lifton concludes that we inhabit a culture of death, characterized by what he describes as 'psychic numbness' – that blunting of the capacity to feel and to experience:

> The image of a destructive force of unlimited dimensions . . . enters into every relationship involving parents, children, grandparents and imagined great grandparents and great grandchildren . . . we are thus among the first to live with a recurrent sense of biological severance.[6]

At a time when CND and the Peace Movement was flourishing, Einstein's words were often quoted. They need repeating now:

> We must never relax our efforts to arouse in the people of the world, especially in their governments, an awareness of the unprecedented disaster which they are absolutely certain to bring on themselves unless there is a fundamental change in their attitudes towards one another as well as in their concept of the future. *The unleashed power of the atom has changed everything except our way of thinking.*

Our consciousness has not changed. We have yet to integrate Hiroshima into our lives so that as the poet Hölderlin says, 'What happens, let all of it be a blessing to you'. This is the sort of faith that tries to omit and forget nothing, to include and never to exclude and to bring everything and everyone, including the worst that we can do, into the forefront of our consciousness and of our experience.

One of the prolonged effects of denial is listlessness, and apathy, the third way of avoidance. It is strange that in a free society, where signals of difficulties and distress are there for all to hear, so many of us remain paralysed. Perhaps it is because to join those who want to make sustainable revolution possible, the cost seems too great.[7] The root cause of apathy is despair, a sense of depression and futility that nothing each of us can do can make any difference. It is a form of frozen violence.

Violence, the fourth way of avoidance, is itself a form of exploding apathy – the desperation to be heard and noticed form the basis of terrorism, and of the mindless savagery of young men raping and killing old women.

Addiction, denial, apathy and violence are a cover-up for the sense that 'we won't make it, and that the future is cancelled'.

Much of this book will be taken up with addressing those techniques of avoidance. I want to show that it is possible to wake up and face the implications of both the sustainable revolution and the nuclear threat, that it is possible to recognize, acknowledge and feel the 'despair' without 'going to pieces', that there are God-given resources for us all to draw on, which means that our experience can after all be trusted. In the experience of transformation of struggle, and of change, we meet the mystery of 'God'. God is not a super power dwelling in a remote heaven from which God intervenes from time to time; nor does God inhabit another realm, another heaven, that stands over against us. For me the meaning of God expresses what is the yet unrealized totality of the world, and the truth of our own lives which are yet to appear. In the struggle over matters of life and death, there is that of the sheer goodness of women and men which is baffling, which has pulled me to my knees, which reveals that 'God' is a presence mediated in and through the struggle luring us into a future into which nothing and no one will lie unredeemed – that 'God may be all in all'.

I have said that organized religion offers comfort and consolation. That is my experience of the Church over many years. There is certainly a place for consolation; even today the Church is the community to which people are drawn because somehow 'everything will be all right'. But we, the clergy, often collude with denial. The matters that I am writing about are not priorities for us: we are busy raising money, bothering about those who we have joined, wishing there were more, trying to keep everyone happy, teaching and preaching and being available. Yet what I am describing is a crisis of the human spirit – a paralysis which has overtaken so many, just when there is so much disintegration and anxiety. The consolations of religion are not enough; we shall retreat further into the shadows, just when we are being called to take our stand with those who are waking up, to make the sustainable revolution work.

Three aspects of our experience are available to motivate, encourage and sharpen the imagination and our knowledge of God. They are (a) voices from the margins, (b) insights from Judaism and reflections on the Holocaust, and (c) a renewed sense of ourselves in relation to nature and creation.

NOTES

1 Emily Dickinson, *Complete Poems*, ed. Thomas H. Johnson (London: Faber and Faber, 1970), p. 644.

2 My high-minded interpretation of Project Apollo needs to be tempered by Norman Mailer's comment that the Project 'was born on the landscape of political machinations, economic cynicism and the manoeuvres of Lyndon Johnson's gravyboat navy'. The material spin-offs from the space project are considerable – micro-circuitry of computers, satellite navigation systems, flameproof car seats, solar batteries, and long-life pacemakers – to name a few.

3. Hans Küng, *Judaism – the Religious Situation of Our Time* (London: SCM Press, 1992), p. 590. Eugene Borowitz is a Rabbi and Professor of Education and Jewish Religious Thought at Hebrew Union College/Jewish Institute of Religion in New York. He is a leading spokesman of American Reform Judaism.

4 The European Values Group – a network of social scientists, theologians, philosophers and opinion researchers.

5 Ngugi Wa Thiongo'o, *Petals of Blood* (London: Heinemann, 1977). Quotation from Robin Richardson, *Daring to Be a Teacher* (Trentham Books, 1990, p. 4); this book should be indispensable for teachers, but offers wisdom, inspiration and delight far beyond the classroom.

6 Robert Jay Lifton, *The Broken Connection* (New York: Simon & Schuster, 1979), p. 338.

7 'Sustainable revolution': the World Commission on Environment and Development describes a sustainable society as one 'that meets the needs of the present without compromising the ability of future generations to meet their own needs': *Our Common Future* (Oxford: OUP, 1987).

   William D. Ruckelhaus asks this question: 'Can we move nations and people in the direction of sustainability? Such a move would be a modification of society comparable in scale to only two other changes: the Agricultural Revolution of the late Neolithic and the Industrial Revolutions of the past two centuries. These revolutions were gradual, spontaneous and largely unconscious. This one will have to be a fully conscious operation, guided by the best foresight that science can provide – if we actually do it, the undertaking will be absolutely unique in humanity's stay on the earth': 'Towards a sustainable world', *Scientific American* (September 1989).

   There is an immense literature on a sustainable society, which is the context out of which *Down to Earth* is written. A useful introduction – with a comprehensive bibliography – is Dennis Meadows and Donella Meadows, *Beyond the Limits – Global Collapse or a Sustainable Future* (London: Earthscan Publications, 1992).

A At the margins

As we attempt to discover how to speak of God, a question arises: 'Who are to be our teachers?' From whom will we seek wisdom and signs of that committed love which will capture the imagination and nourish our own commitment?

There are no simple answers to these questions and there are certainly no available blueprints. But the hint of an answer comes from the margins, from those voices – millions of them – who are nevertheless on the edge of society. In the 1970s and 1980s, a new movement emerged in the Roman Catholic Church in some parts of Central and South America, known as liberation theology. It has often been admired in the USA, Europe and the United Kingdom, but because our circumstances are so different, it has had little or no effect on the life of our society or churches.

Liberation theology, and the practice which it both reflects and nourishes, begins with reality. Christopher Rowland in *Radical Christianity* describes this reality:

A reality of poverty, appalling living conditions – contrasting with the affluence not only of the First World, but even more glaring still, with the wealth and splendour of the upper middle-class accommodation of Latin American cities. A visit to a *favela* on the periphery of São Paulo in Brazil will give a glimpse of that reality which makes any semblance of a solution for the thousands living without proper homes and facilities seem light years away. By way of contrast there are luxurious apartments in the well-protected condominiums often standing cheek by jowl with a *favela* which put the life-style of the North American and European middle class in the shade. It is that discrepancy between the gross affluence of the tiny minority and the demeaning squalor which the majority have to endure that has prompted many Christians to think again about their apostolic task, and in doing so they have learned the importance of living and working with, and above all learning from, the poor.[1]

This learning began and begins with a process of what is known as 'conscientization'.[2] It is a process of aiding those whose suffering has been so intense that they have been struck dumb to bring their experience into speech, to break the silence, to understand their situation, and co-operatively to transform it. This is the first step in the process of liberation. A story told of the revolutionary Che Guevara puts it simply – he said that he and his men were accused of going into the villages, raping the women and shooting the men, and burning their homes. He said this was not so. What they did was to gather the people together, and invite them to tell the stories of their lives and to listen to them, and that was the start of the Revolution.

The gathering together of people in small communities is an essential part of this process. (There are thousands of such groups in Brazil.) Here, little deference is paid to experts, the experience of each is honoured, and the community is a means by which each person is affirmed. As everywhere else, these base communities have their share of real difficulties – fierce arguments and disagreements, but to some they are a glimpse of what the new Church and the new world could be like.

Base communities, as they are known, meet together to reflect on their experience, and in many different ways are involved in projects, or act as catalysts for projects for the Church and society. Thus, at a meeting of the base communities at Goiana in 1986, the report of 1,500 representatives from the 100,000 base communities describes the activities of the people's movement:

> The people's movement has many rivers – the river of the trade unions, the river of the political parties, the river of the neighbourhood groups, the river of the landless movement, of the slumdwellers, of marginalised women, of fishers, of the aged, of the physically handicapped, of children, of women, of blacks, of the Indian nations . . . But the struggles recounted here show that they are growing all over Brazil; struggles of resistance are becoming struggles of conquest. The people's political project will channel the waters of all these rivers into one great river that will finally do away with the society of wealth and oppression and lay foundations for the kind of society God wants.[3]

The lifeblood of these communities is prayer, the sacraments, and particularly the Bible, which nourishes their hope and casts light on their own experience – not the experience of the inner life, but the primary text of their everyday lives. The experience of God among the poor, inspired by the radical Jesus and his teachings about the Kingdom, and of a God leading the people to a promised land is enriching and sustaining; and sustenance is something to be cherished in most Latin American countries where reactionary forces are still firmly in place, even where some form of democracy has been established. The new Jerusalem is a long way off.

What is happening in liberation thinking and practice is a dynamic way of handling experience: it is a way of speaking, seeing, guiding and acting, or of learning by doing, or of analysing, acting, reflecting and singing (celebration if you like). All this learning is circular and continuous. I have been lucky enough to meet women and men who have been part of these base communities, or who have been inspired by them, or who have written about them, and been changed by them. Without exception, such people generate vitality and life which is a striking contrast to so many comfortable and tired church communities in Britain!

Liberation theology growing out of the experience of the poor is only a fraction of the life of the Roman Catholic Church in most Latin American countries, except in Brazil; and it has been greeted only grudgingly by the Vatican.

The experience of the poor is central to our concern in this chapter. By the 'poor' I mean precisely those who in Britain today are called the underclass. They are unwanted, written off, marginalized. They are regarded as useless.[4]

Until very recently the 'workers' were organized around the raw materials of production. A considerable workforce was required to create manufacturing industries. Now the working classes are regarded primarily as consumers. Consumers are needed to serve the goals of an acquisitive society. The more that is consumed, so that argument goes, the more healthy the economy. Those who have little prospect of becoming consumers (for whatever reason) are the 'underclass'. They pose no threats. They are not organized. They are 'invisible' people, surplus to requirements. Their oppression is economic, and cultural. After all, if the fundamental values of a society are based on competition and acquisition values, reinforced by education, the media and politicians, then it is unthinkable to conceive of any alternative.

Yet there are alternatives. In the Gospels, Jesus places himself among the equivalent of our underclass. They were at the centre of his life. The awkward, specific and radical nature of his life is so easily lost. From that centre, Jesus speaks about the Kingdom of God. He quite clearly identifies two areas of their experience which kept the people down – one was the demands of ritual purity, the other was the debt structure. Jesus ignored all the complex regulations (mostly about diet and sex) which had to be obeyed before being accepted by God. None of these were necessary. (In the first chapters of Mark there are many stories of Jesus at war with the ideology of the purity rules – curing Peter's mother-in-law and then eating with her, raising up the girl in puberty, and the woman whose blood had indicated impurity.) He made a point of eating and drinking with those who were regarded as unclean – tax collectors and sinners. These meals are powerful symbols. They signify an intimacy and respect for those with whom Jesus ate and drank, which inevitably led to clashes with the rigid and hierarchical society.

The poor were not just excluded because of their 'unworthiness'. The poor were also nearly destroyed by debts. The debt structures of Jesus' day, like our own, were most destructive. The poor were heavily taxed and responsible for tithes to help with the upkeep of Jerusalem. Loans were absolutely essential if they were to survive the strictures of the law, which prevented them working on the Sabbath, even though their debts were increasing. And to that unjust structure which made and kept the poorest so guilty, so imprisoned, Jesus lifts the burden and says 'Your sins are forgiven'. The priests were permitted to release people from debt, but Jesus takes that authority to do that for himself, and includes anyone who accepts that authority. And from that centre, he provides hope and a glimpse of a new future.

Today the underclass are confronted and punished by the debts they cannot and should not pay. They do not borrow money to buy luxury items; they owe phenomenal debts at exorbitant rates for their survival.

Thus I imagine Jesus choosing to be among those who suffer as a result of their debt. Even now I can hear him (just) talking about the good news of release to the captives. I hear him teaching his friends to pray:

> 'Forgive us our debts
> as we also have forgiven our debtors.'

I recognize even after 2,000 years that in his eating and drinking with his friends he is showing that those on the edge of society belong with us and we with them. I move closer and hear his call for repentance directed at me, and any who will listen; we are to discover a new fellowship with the underclass. As I listen I 'hear the cry of our brothers' blood, crying out to God from the earth'.

The message is clear: the first becomes last, and the last first. And the last will discover their confidence, their strength and their hope. It is then that the struggle begins. In the Book of Revelation there is a struggle between the great beast of the Roman Empire in all its riches, luxury, magnificence and power, and the 'Lamb that was slain' – an innocent, vulnerable community which through the eyes of faith will ultimately bring down the Beast. God's promises will be vindicated.

These last paragraphs are the stuff of sermons; it would be hard to fault their basis as biblical texts. But there is little sign of that struggle between the churches and society; hardly a sense of the often battered inner-city communities as being engaged in a struggle for the transformation of the world: the rhetoric of the Bible at this point has yet to be rooted in practice.

There is another question: how does liberation theology affect the middle classes who constitute most of the church membership? The problem with the question is that we do not recognize our own oppression. Some Christians feel a sense of guilt for their relative affluence. Guilt leads to the conclusion that we are guilty, because we chose to be affluent. And since we ourselves created the problems we can therefore alleviate them. We are free to do so.

But that is not the case. We may feel guilty, but we are also powerless. We establish projects, fix what we can. For many years, like many city-centre churches, St James's, Piccadilly, has been concerned to 'do something about and for the homeless'. Modest activities have been started, and then abandoned. Sooner or later, we encounter our own powerlessness because we discover that we are caught up in a society which wishes to maintain the *status quo*. To consider any alternative is almost out of the question. The middle-class Christian is not a free agent. She may be comfortable, and be in a position to make limited choices about her life, but when it comes to struggling for radical change, she soon discovers how little can be done (which is not to say that what little can be done should not be done).

In the 1980s this analysis was invariably regarded and dismissed as the Church involving itself in politics. What is often forgotten is that the tradition to curb the power and greed of the powerful, and to protect and care for the weakest in the community, is the heart of Judaism, and of the life of Jesus Christ. It is an ancient and venerable tradition which goes back some 3,000 years to the extraordinary events (recorded in Exodus 19) on Mount Sinai, when God establishes the decrees which will shape his new relationship with his people – in what is known as the Ten Commandments. On Mount Sinai, God's massive presence intrudes. God's holiness is revealed in the terror, splendour and inscrutability of God's 'appearance'. The awe of this moment moves to the offer of covenant: God will be known now as the God of Israel who will care for, and preside over, the life of Israel. The shape of this new relationship is revealed in the Ten Commandments or the Ten Words, as they are more correctly known. The Commandments are an embarrassment to Christians. They are stark, awkward, uncompromising and non-negotiable.

As in many seventeenth-century churches, St James's, Piccadilly has two frames on which the Commandments are printed – gold lettering on a black background. They have been moved to various parts of the church at different times, but never quite thrown out or destroyed. In the nineteenth century, they were hung above the altar. When the church was rebuilt after its bombing in the war, the frames were moved to a discreet place in the lobbies. Then, later, when the lobbies were decorated, they were moved out of sight to the organ loft. There they remain. What is to be done with the Ten Commandments?

Some see them as having no use – suitable directions for a primitive agricultural community, but of no value for today. (Feminist theologians have noted that women were excluded from the Sinai event;[5] and today there needs to be yet another commandment 'Thou shalt love the Earth, etc.'!!) More usually they are reduced to those matters which vex our Western introspective conscience: thus 'Thou shalt not covet' becomes an admonition to be neither jealous nor envious.

But the Commandments are a blueprint of what an ideal community should be. They provide the ground rules for public policy and institutional life.

The first three Commandments speak of the holiness of God. God cannot be captured, domesticated, conformed to our arrangements. The God who delivered the slaves from Egypt is free, and a dangerous God, not to be trivialized or reduced. The Commandments are a reminder of that perception of reality which acknowledges the Other, an inscrutable mystery which cannot be seduced or possessed. The last six Commandments balance the holiness of God with the humanity of the community. To recognize the 'Other' is to draw a line against all brutality and any action which violates the dignity of the neighbour. The elderly – the father and mother – are to be honoured, not because they have earned their place, but just because they belong. Every member of the community is to be given life: 'Do not kill.' Binding loyalties are taken with great seriousness: 'Do not commit adultery.' The weakest are not to be taken into debt slavery: 'You shall not steal.' And old land boundaries are to be honoured, and not removed by commercial practices: 'Do not covet.'

Those who scoff at liberation theology betray an astonishing ignorance of the core, the kernel, of Judaism, disclosed in Jesus Christ, and wherever in history these intuitions are lived out. The dignity of humanity is matched exactly by honouring God. And if there are those in Central America who have known something of the transcendence of God, then it can be the same for us in Britain.

From time to time I have made occasions for people to learn the methodology of liberation theology. I call these courses 'Doing theology'; I promise to turn anyone who participates into a theologian; and if they are not satisfied their fee will be refunded! I do not mean theologians in an academic sense, but in the sense of making connections between faith and life. Everyone has an opportunity to tell their story, reflect on it, consider those aspects of it which hinder, constrain or block their lives, and come to some proposals for action. Often those who come have little in common with each other, except to have the opportunity of participating; a lack of a common identity is sometimes a disadvantage in that the group cannot easily work together, but the diversity of interest provides an opportunity for the members to encourage one another.

While it is absurd to claim too much for these modest learning experiments, I have noticed several consistent themes. One is dissatisfaction with whatever church they were or had been associated with; the dissatisfaction is always expressed in the same way – that their life experiences were not taken seriously enough by their communities. Another was the language that is used to speak about their faith and beliefs. To assist this process I invited everyone to make a list in a random manner of everything they associated with 'religion', 'Christianity' and 'Church'. It has been rare to find someone who is comfortable with the professional, theological language of the clergy. It has been salutary to recognize that most lay persons, however badly or well educated, speak about their faith and religious experience not from sermons or theological books but from carols, hymns, stories and phrases from the Bible and elsewhere.

Religious energy, or a renewed sense of God, begins to blossom where a person begins to become aware of some deep unmet need within herself; as the connections are made with the images and stories, so it is possible to speak of a renewed vitality, a new awareness of God's grace beckoning her forward.

Therefore, there need to be many opportunities where we can help one another to move from silence to speech. There need to be places of trust where unheard-of stories and experience can emerge. Knowledge is generally understood as one person wielding power over others in the interests of detachment, disengagement and objectivity. But there is another knowledge which emerges from the narratives of the elderly, the chronically sick, the mentally handicapped, the sexually disfranchised, ethnic minorities, prisoners, the unemployed, the experiences of many women and those who speak to us on behalf of the pain of the earth. All of us, not least those in the middle and professional classes, need to engage in that process of conscientization, and tell our stories, as we discover we are part of that same society, that same system which disfranchises and subdues so many.

What emerges from these gatherings, which take place over a period of time, is their humanity. There may be tears, but there is also laughter; there is often a sharp disagreement, but when members listen well to one another, those disagreements can be held. At its best, these experiences have a celebratory quality about them.

What possibilities there are for forming networks, coalitions and communities of every sort in which there is good listening, imaginative learning, reaching, touching, cherishing and remembering! If liberation theology can work in Brazil, then, as I know from my own life, it can happen here – wherever two or three are gathered together.

There is not yet sufficient evidence, sufficient experience to describe the effect of this method of living, reflecting, and celebrating, but I suspect

what will begin to emerge is a degree of nonconformity and social heroism.[6]
Walt Whitman conveys what I mean:

> This is what you should do: love the earth and sun and the animals,
> despise riches, give alms to everyone that asks, stand up for the stupid
> and crazy, devote your income and labour to others, hate tyrants, argue
> not concerning God, have patience and indulgence toward the people,
> take off your hat to nothing known or unknown or to any man or
> number of men ... re-examine all you have been told at school
> or church or in any book, dismiss what insults your own soul, and your
> very flesh shall be a great poem.

NOTES

1 Christopher Rowland, *Radical Christianity* (Cambridge: Polity Press, 1988), p. 116.
2 'Conscientization' from Paulo Freire, *Pedagogy of the Oppressed* (Harmondsworth: Penguin Books, 1972). My point will be that the same method of 'education' can work in middle-class communities.
3 *Radical Christianity*, p. 121. I am aware that the practice of liberation theology is now more discredited – but its methodology and passion for a new future is still timely.
4 I have drawn freely on Laurie Green's unpublished paper 'Freed for the future: debt and the underclass' for this consideration of Jesus and the poor.
5 Exodus 19. See Judith Plaskow, *Standing Again at Sinai: Judaism from a Feminist Perspective* (San Francisco: HarperSanFrancisco, 1991).
6 'Social heroism' – a phrase which emerges as a characteristic of those from middle classes who practise liberation. See Paul King, Kent Maynard and David Woodward, *Risking Liberation – Middle Class Powerlessness and Social Heroism* (Atlanta: John Knox Press, 1988).

B   Between the fires[1]

Night is an autobiographical account of a Jewish boy's experience of the death camps. Its author, Elie Wiesel, was given the Nobel Peace Prize in 1986, and in the presentation ceremony the chairman, Egil Aarik, said: 'From the abyss of the death camps he has come as a messenger to mankind ... not with a message of hate and revenge, but with one of brotherhood and atonement.'[2] *Night* is, on Wiesel's own account, the centre of all his subsequent writing, and central to considering the question 'Where is God?'

Night is a reversal of the tradition of the Exodus and Sinai. The covenant is broken; God did not deliver his people; humanity turned away. As in the Exodus, there is a 'going out', not to the promised land but to chaos into the horror of the death camps. It was Passover again, but this time the Angel of Death did not spare the Jewish children. The Jews of Sighet (Elie Wiesel's home town in what was Transylvania, with a population of 10,000 Jews) are taken to a place where the food tastes like dead bodies, where children are hung on the gallows, and people ask 'Where is God?' Instead of Moses leading the people through the desert where God provided every need, there is only the dark smoke of the crematoria against the background of a silent blue sky.

The Holocaust destroys once and for all traditional belief in an intervening and miracle-working God. The belief that there is a God, all good, all knowing, all powerful and everywhere present, and intervening to protect the innocent, cannot survive Auschwitz (or all the acts of genocide and mass murders which this century has witnessed). In Dostoevsky's *Brothers Karamazov*, Ivan Karamazov says that he had to return his ticket to God because of the sufferings of one child. What would he have said of the deaths of six million innocent Jews – a Holocaust at which Christianity had colluded? As Hitler said to two Roman Catholic bishops who were complaining about his treatment of the Jews, 'I am finishing off what you yourselves started'.[3]

The Holocaust urges the question again and again – Where is God? Is there any way at all in which places of such suffering mediate a religious response, so that it is possible to speak of God and to call on God?

The beginnings of an answer lie in a poem by Arthur Waskow:

We are the generation
That stands between the fires.
Behind us is the flame and smoke
That rose from Auschwitz and from Hiroshima.
Before us is the nightmare of a Flood of Fire;
A thermonuclear holocaust
That could make every human city
A crematorium without a chimney.
It is our task to make from fire
Not an all-consuming blaze
But the light in which we see each other;
All of us different,
All of us made in the image of God.
We light this fire to see more clearly
That the earth, the human race, is not for burning.
We light this fire to see more clearly
The rainbow in our many-colored faces.[4]

Like the poets I stand between two fires – those of Hiroshima and Auschwitz linked together by the threat they now present for the future. Unlike the poet, I am a Christian not a Jew, but I have been profoundly affected by the way many survivors of the Holocaust and Jewish writers (and some Christians) have reacted to it. The surprise of the poem lies in the transition from the flames of Auschwitz and Hiroshima and the prospect of a Flood of Fire to something else:

> It is our task to make from fire
> Not an all-consuming blaze
> But the light in which we see each other.

This is an astounding challenge: to put life before death and transform the memory of fire to an occasion for life and liberation – 'To see more clearly the rainbow in our many-coloured faces'. This mysterious movement of the human spirit – the making of a choice to live – can easily be reduced, trivialized or explained away, but to do it justice I would want to speak of God as its source, strength and possibility.

But it is not easy (or just a solution) to speak of God. A clue to understanding how faith – in this context – works is to consider the Jewish tradition of *chutzpah*. This, in the words of Beldon Lane is:

an audacious faith, almost bordering on insolence that stalks the high country of belief and disbelief. It seems especially prevalent in the rarefied air above Mt Sinai. Rooted deeply in the human experience of adversity and anguish, it opens onto a landscape where God and human beings walk as friends, 'Chutzpa k'lapei shamaya' it is called in the Jewish tradition – a boldness with regard to heaven. From Moses, the Psalmist, and Jeremiah to such rabbinical figures as Honi the Circle Drawer in the first century BCE – from Levi-Yitzhaq of Berditchev in the hasidic world of Eastern Europe to the pain-soaked novels of Elie Wiesel – it echoes through the Jewish past with a stubborn insistence.[5]

In Judaism, the covenant between God and God's people established a relationship between two parties. The people had to live by God's Commandments, and God had obligations to be with his people. It was and is a two-way process. The suffering of the Jewish people, especially at its most intense, provoked among its poets, prophets and teachers, anger, despair, audacity, familiarity and defiance.

The Book of Job illustrates the boldness of humanity with regard to heaven. Job was a model of piety. His family, health and property are all taken away from him. His friends try and comfort him, saying that really Job must be guilty and deserves everything that happens to him. Job (in chapter 3) is angry and defiant, and wants to put God on trial – but he knows that even if such a trial was to happen it would not be fair, for 'He would crush me with a tempest' (9.15–18). Sure enough, this happens when God eventually responds to Job's challenge. Job repents. And just as the story ends, everything is turned upside down. God says to the comforters, 'You have not in fact told the truth'. Job did. Job wrestled with God, and Job won the battle. God casts doubt on his own behaviour to defend the dignity of Job against the false piety of his friends (who wanted to make Job guilty in order to make God appear just).

The Book of Job is not a theological treatise on the relationship between God and injustice, but it does affirm a primary theme of *chutzpah*, which is that human dignity always must prevail (whatever God does).

The best biblical story that conveys *chutzpah* is, of course, that of Jacob wrestling with the stranger. Jacob is on his way home to Canaan; he is now a considerable man of substance, but he is worried about Esau's reaction to him. He sends his retinue of wives and children and servants ahead. Jacob is alone. A stranger appears. They wrestle until daybreak. The stranger is inscrutable. Jacob asks for a blessing. The stranger, who wants to leave for it is almost day, asks Jacob his name. Jacob tells him, and the stranger names him 'Israel, for you have striven with God and with humans and have prevailed'. Still the stranger refuses to tell Jacob his name, but he receives the blessing, and Jacob realizes he has been wrestling with God and that he has survived. He is left limping, wounded in the thigh.

This is the account of a Promethean battle. But who is the stranger? Is it an ancient tale of a river spirit trying to prevent a traveller from crossing? Is it his brother, Esau, in disguise? Esau is certainly on his mind, and when he meets Esau the next day Jacob says 'Truly, to see your face is like seeing the face of God!' Perhaps. But the story gives some hints. The stranger will not be identified; he will not give his name. He must leave before he can be seen. But he gives Jacob a new name – so that a new being is called forth, and he blesses Jacob. It is as if the person is God.

What does it mean to say that Jacob wrestles with God? The one who protects and promises (as in the dream of Jacob's ladder) is also the one with whom Jacob fights all night long; it is like discovering that the detective is the murderer.

During the night wrestling, the reader becomes part of that struggle, struggling, clamouring like Jacob with his desperate questions to be recognized by God who yet remains unreachable. Like Jacob we struggle, at least for a blessing so that some new thing will come from this mysterious encounter. The reader has followed Jacob from his birth; now Jacob is set to return to Canaan – but in his wrestling, we are momentarily part of Jacob himself; we are inside his soul, wrestling as Jacob on every side, reaching out as Jacob, questioning as Jacob, grasping as Jacob, not letting go as Jacob.

And then the narrative resumes. 'The sun rose upon him, as he passed Penuel, limping because of his hip.' We become the readers from a more distant viewpoint watching this limping man, who has yet seen God face to face, walking now in front of his wives and servants and children to meet Esau, who, for reasons we will never know, runs to meet him, embraces him, kisses him, 'and they wept'.

Both in the Talmudic tradition and the mystical-Hasidic traditions, faith as *chutzpah* is expressed in countless stories:

> One day the Hasidic master Rabbi Levi-Yitzhaq of Berditchev asked a poor tailor to speak of the argument he had had with God that day in his prayers. The tailor responded:

> > 'I told the Master of the Universe . . . today is the Day of Judgment. One must repent. But I didn't sin much. I took a little left-over cloth from the rich. I once drank a glass of brandy and ate some bread without washing my hands. These are all my transgressions. But *You*, Master of the Universe, how many are *Your* transgressions? You have taken away small children who had not sinned. From others you have taken away the mothers of such children. But, Master of the Universe, I shall forgive You Your transgressions, You forgive mine, and let us drink *L'Hayyim* (to life)!'

> That year Reb Levi-Yitzhaq proclaimed that it was this tailor with his argument who had saved the Jews. 'Ah,' he added, 'but if *I* had been in his place, I would not have forgiven the Master of the World such great sins in return for a little leftover cloth. While I had Him, I would have asked that He send us His Messiah to redeem the World!'[6]

Had Judaism developed a systematic, metaphysical theology, providing answers to fundamental religious questions like 'What is the meaning of life?' or 'Why do people suffer?', then it is possible that Judaism might well have disappeared as a living tradition after the Holocaust, but because Jewish faith is grounded in covenant, dialogue and wrestling with God, it continues. Elie Wiesel's work can only be understood in the light of this tradition. So he says:

There were many periods in our past when we had every right in the world to turn to God and say, 'Enough. Since you seem to approve of all these persecutions, all these outrages, have it Your way: let Your world go on without Jews. Either You are our partner in history, or You are not. If you are, do your share; if You are not, we consider ourselves free of past commitments. Since you choose to break the covenant, so be it.' And yet, and yet . . . We went on believing, hoping, invoking His name. In the endless engagement with God, we proved to Him that we were more patient than He, more compassionate, too. In other words, we did not give up on Him either. For this is the essence of being Jewish; never to give up – never to yield to despair.

Or again:

As far as belief in God is concerned I would simply suggest to question Him and go on questioning Him *through* such belief. In doing so one remains within certain limits and within a certain tradition, namely the Jewish tradition.[7]

Wiesel's argument is well put in his repeated teaching of the Hasidic master Rebbe Baruch of Nedzehozh:

I know there are questions that have no answers; there is a suffering that has no name; there is injustice in God's creation – and there are reasons enough for man to explode with rage. I know there are reasons for you to be angry. Good. Let us be angry. Together.

Stories and quotations from this tradition give a slight flavour of *chutzpah*, so strange to Christian ears. In the Warsaw Ghetto, these words were scrawled on a wall:

> I believe in the sun when it doesn't shine.
> I believe in love when I cannot feel it.
> I believe in God, even when I do not see Him.

The people in Auschwitz did not cry to a weak, helpless, dead God. As they prayed, and many did, they will have cried to a living God who was absent, one in whom they trusted. This tough faith, a mass of logical contradictions, is always an expression of faith in a God who desires and champions the dignity of men and women.

Christianity knows little of the *chutzpah* tradition. There are echoes of it in the gospels and in the words of Jesus on the cross, 'My God, my God, why have you forsaken me?' In writings on prayer and the inner life, there are those who speak of wrestling with God, but the contest is required to end in submission.

Submission and trust are the dominant traditions in Christianity. The tradition of lament, for example, is missing entirely from prayer and worship. I have never experienced in Christian liturgy a sense of passionate longing and impatience with God; our intercessions sound like so many 'sound bites' filling in God with the news and the current black spots in the world. The anaemic quality of so much Christian worship needs to learn from this bold *chutzpah* tradition. Christians have been prepared to be just 'bearers of sufferings' or 'sharing the sufferings of Christ'. Christianity has been too much identified with the prosperous and comfortable to hear these voices from Judaism.

But a religion which puts trust, submission and obedience to God first and last suffers not just in liturgy but in its failure to take 'history' seriously: the realities and challenges of immense suffering in the world. The Austrian Catholic philosopher Friedrich Heer writes:

The withdrawal of the church from history has created that specifically Christian and ecclesiastical irresponsibility towards the world, the Jew, the other person, even the Christian himself, considered as a human being – which was the ultimate cause of past catastrophes and could well be the cause of a final catastrophe in the future.[8]

As the implications of the sustainable revolution begin to be addressed, and some of the apparently intractable problems are brought out into the open, the *chutzpah* tradition is something to be discovered and employed in worship and in life. I have been writing about what has mostly been a man's world; I am not aware of a tradition of *chutzpah* among Jewish women, and not – perhaps until recently among feminist poets and theologians – of something similar in Christianity; so let the poet Annie Dillard have the last word. She wrestles with the story of Moses, she peers with bloodshot eyes from within the 'cleft' of the rock, waiting for the passing of God. Her words summarize all the risk, muttered longing and playful trust that *chutzpa k'lapei shamaya* affords:

You can pursue him wherever you dare, risking the shrunken sinew in the hollow of the thigh; you can bang at the door all night till the innkeeper relents, if he ever relents; and you can wail till you're hoarse or worse the cry for incarnation always in John Knoepfle's poem: 'and

Christ is red rover . . . and the children are calling / come over come over.' I sit on a bridge as on Pisgah and banging with all my will, calling like a child beating on a door; Come on out! . . . I know you're there.[9]

NOTES

1 The inspiration for 'Between the fires' comes from papers presented at an international scholars' conference held in 1988 in Oxford: *Remembering for the Future – Jews and Christians During and After the Holocaust* (Oxford: Pergamon Press, 1988).
2 Fred L. Downing, 'Autobiography, fiction and faith – reflections on the literary and religious pilgrimage of Elie Wiesel' in *Remembering for the Future*, p. 1441.
3 Rosemary Radford Ruether cites the story of Hitler's 'Tabletalk' in *Faith and Fratricide* (New York: Seabury Press, 1979), pp. 223 and 224.
4 Arthur Waskow, 'Between the fires' from *The Shalom Seders: Three Haggadahs*, compiled by the New Jewish Agenda (New York: Adama Books, 1984); quoted in Henry Knight, 'Choosing life between the fires: towards an intentionalist voice of faith' in *Remembering for the Future*, p. 637.
5 Belden Lane, 'Hutzpa k'lapei schamay – a Christian response to the Jewish tradition of arguing with God', *Journal of Ecumenical Studies*, vol. 23, no. 4 (Fall 1986), pp. 567 and 568; quoted by Darrell Fasching, 'Faith and ethics after the Holocaust' in *Remembering for the Future*, p. 599.
6 Raphael Patai, *Gate to the Old City* (New York: Avon Books, 1980), cited in Lane, 'Hutzpa k'lapei schamay', p. 581; quoted by Darrell Fasching, 'Faith and ethics', p. 600.
7 Elie Wiesel, *The Trial of God* (New York: Schocken Books, 1979), from the Introduction entitled 'The scene'.
8 Friedrich Heer, quoted by John Pawlikowski in *Remembering for the Future*, Theme 1, p. 743.
9 Annie Dillard, *Pilgrim at Tinker Creek* (New York: Bantam Books, 1975), p. 209.

C Nature

All are but parts of one stupendous whole
Whose body Nature is and God the soul.
Pope (*Essay on Man*)

Some years ago I took some American friends on a church crawl in Gloucestershire, Shropshire and Wales. It was a disappointing drive, since all the churches I wanted to show my friends were locked. We completed our tour in the early evening by visiting the ruins of Tintern Abbey.

I remember the intensity and vividness of the 'greenness' of the sur-
roundings of the Abbey. The stained glass windows had long been ripped
out, and were filled with the green of the hills. The roof and its beams
had gone, and the evening sun streamed in. After our failure to gain access
to any church building, I wondered why I had bothered. Here at Tintern,
like a pagan temple, nature was neither ignored nor shut out, but provided
a natural and most appropriate setting for worship.

One of the difficulties that arises in trying to speak naturally and easily
about God and nature is that we have no ready language, no framework
in which such discourse can take place. By nature, I mean that part of
it which predates the human species; it is a vast, living infrastructure
of organizations tightly coupled with their environment to create a living
planet. In the interests of progress and freedom, or just simply an attempt
to make life better, nature, on which our very existence depends, has been
abused and defiled. Those 'closed' churches were closed to the natural
world. Mainstream Christianity has been a silent partner in this abuse.
Because nature is non-human, it is easily regarded as unredeemable, inanimate and incapable of reflecting the divine presence. After all, there
is no need to concern ourselves with these conundrums if nature is an
apparently inexhaustible reservoir out of which raw materials can be used
for our own purposes.

But that narrow perception is now being challenged: faced with our
capacity to break mountains, remove forests, drain rivers, flood valleys,
create dust bowls, pollute the air, fill rivers with sewage and the oceans with
oil and nuclear waste, where among all this devastation and plundering
is God?

There is no ready answer to this question because we have so long been
autistic in our relationship to the natural world. We are a highly intelligent
species, but beyond the plundering cannot relate easily, or intelligently, to
nature. 'Pagan temple' was the best I could do to describe the way in which
the ruins of Tintern – allowing nature to flood in – were, for me, the ideal
setting for worship, even more so than some of those locked village churches
where once inside and the door closed, the natural world is shut out.

It may be too rapid a transition from perceiving nature as inanimate,
to perceiving it as a divine, living organism, but at least it could be desirable to establish a relationship of courtesy and respect towards it. There is
a possibility of developing attitudes to nature as one of give and take,
apologizing for our intrusion as and when we have to. Our human world
is not self-contained. Our relationship with the environment has an
ethical, and a religious, dimension. Sacrilege is not just a word used to
describe vandalizing a graveyard.

Like many others, I have begun to learn from tribal people about attitudes to the natural world which are neither romantic nor sentimental but reflect their own instinct for survival.

In a museum at the edge of Death Valley in California, there is a drawing of three native American Indians – from the Shoshone tribe – peering over some rocks in amazement at a procession of huge wagons, and immense oxen driven by black-suited, pale-faced, God-fearing Protestant prospectors from the East Coast: they had come to California to look for gold. Death Valley is one of the most inhospitable places on earth, where there is little rain, temperatures of 120 degrees or more, and hardly any water. Yet for 400 years the Indians had survived and lived in that desert. Their look of disbelief at the Americans from the East arose because they knew that they would not survive. And they were right. Not only did these frontier men and women exterminate the Indians, or as many as they could, but they themselves died in such an alien landscape. Tourists today can see remains of these 'gold cities'.

Nature, for those Indians, was regarded with trepidation. It was a mystery on which lay their survival. They recognized that unpredictable and chaotic as nature could be, it, like a great mother, gave life to them. It therefore had to be treated with respect and courtesy.

It is, of course, impossible to know what such tribal people 'felt' or experienced. But certainly it was never as childish or stupid as Christian missionaries have made it to be: 'The heathen in his blindness bows down to wood and stone' as Bishop Heber's hymn puts it;[1] even as he was writing this hymn the cotton mills in Manchester were filling the skies with soot. The savages, whoever they were, were regarded as backward and superstitious, much in need of Christianity and civilizing (or extermination – if that failed).

It is doubtful if these tribal people understood the 'stones' they worshipped as divine – more likely that everything was transparent with their gods, who needed appeasing, entreating, as well as praising. Today it is a sign of generous souls who will seek instruction about nature and the gods, wherever it can be found.[2]

Tribal peoples had their creation stories; they knew how their world had come to be, and how they fitted into it. We have no creation story. Thomas Berry writes:

Our traditional story of the universe sustained us for a long period of time. It shaped our emotional attitudes, provided us with life purposes, and energized action. It consecrated suffering and integrated knowledge. We awoke in the morning and knew who we were . . . It did provide a context in which life could function in a meaningful manner.[3]

The Christian creation story received its first blow from Galileo. His discovery that the earth was only one of six known planets circling round the sun destroyed not just the accepted cosmology, but all the hierarchical thinking which taught it. Then Darwin showed that man and woman did not just appear, as in Genesis, but were the product of a long evolution. And contemporary scientists are unravelling the mysteries of the universe.

As the amazing story of the creation of the universe, fifteen billion years ago, is retold, our attention is drawn not merely to the physical process by which the universe, the planet and life on the planet came into being, but by the ways in which every aspect of life and the development of life itself are dependent on each other. The balance of this creative process has been so fine, so delicate, that were it disturbed, creation itself is endangered.

An example of such disturbance is the extinction of dinosaurs – which had ruled the earth for 160 million years – some 65 million years ago, for reasons which are not clear. It could possibly have been that the earth was hit by an asteroid, creating such a dust storm that the sun's rays were unable to reach the earth, decimating the flora and fauna; but the extinction of dinosaurs created the space for the next transformation – proliferation of mammals out of which emerged a prototype of the human species – the great apes – some four million years ago.

Only now are we beginning to grasp the sequence of transformation in the universe, shaping the galaxies, and fashioning the elements, gathering the solar system with its multitude of planets, churning together the materials that make up the Earth, shaping our seas and continents, the atmosphere and its oxygen and then slowly the coming of life in its astounding diversity – from plants and animals, from the simplest virus, to the eventual emerging of the human species and the subsequent developments across the planet.

At the end of *The Universe Story*, Brian Swimme and Thomas Berry write:

> The important thing to appreciate is that the story (of the universe) is not the story of a mechanistic, essentially meaningless universe but the story of a universe that has from the beginning had its mysterious self-organizing power that if experienced in any serious moment, must evoke an even greater sense of awe than that evoked in earlier times at the experience of the dawn breaking over the horizon, the lightning storm crashing over the hills, or the night sound of the tropical rain forests, for it is out of this story that all of these phenomena emerged.[4]

The cosmic story needs to be told then not just in a reductionist, mechanistic manner, as if that sort of analytic knowledge was the only way to know anything, but by scientists, poets, the shamans of ancient religious traditions, women and mystics in ways that evoke from us awe, reverence and love – a love which will call us to the awesome task of healing and sustaining the earth. Thus the primary source of life is the earth itself and the health of us all depends on the health of the planet. The primary and essential mode of the disclosure of God is in nature itself, which as we have seen, invites courtesy and attention. That is why Thomas Berry writes: 'We cannot do without the traditional religions, but they cannot presently do what needs to be done. We need a new type of religious orientation'[5] – that which perceives and experiences nature, or the earth as the primary sacrament of the love and presence of God.

However, the trouble with this perception of God is that life is not readily experienced like that. If it is argued that there is a fundamental unity which holds us all together, amidst our diversity and the interdependence of everything, it is rare to experience it. Rare, but not impossible, as I know from my own life. Shortly after my mother died I had such an experience.

My mother died in much pain; she had a malignant tumour in the brain. After her death at home, I felt the need to get out of the house and also to discuss the funeral arrangements. I went to visit an aunt and uncle who lived in a long, low Sussex flintstone farm house. As I turned the corner, I suddenly had to stop the car. I got out, and sat on the verge. Their house was at the end of a lane, and there was no traffic. Every window in the house was open. The front door was open. I noticed the sheep in the orchard, especially Mary, the ewe, fatter than all the others, because she was a pet. I saw the peacocks in the gardens, a swan on the pond in front of the house. It was a warm, sunny day and the three spaniels belonging to my uncle were asleep outside the front door. They looked up when they saw me. I had stopped the car because at that moment I felt completely at one with what I had seen; it was as if my whole world had fitted together. It evoked from me a sense of completeness, wonder and awe. As it faded I experienced an overwhelming sadness, not just at the loss of my mother, but at this experience which had been taken away from me. I knew that there was something unfinished about those moments. But it was the unity of everything which remains.

Whenever I have shared this experience, I discover that I am not alone – that in fact such experiences in all their vividness and oddness are commonplace. The Alister Hardy Research Centre at Westminster College, Oxford, which collects and studies religious experience, endorses my own.

But there are difficulties with such 'moments' – one is that organized religion is superior about them or fears them and does not wish to integrate them in any way, thus reinforcing a sense that Christianity is a closed system, rejecting the many varieties of religious experience. The other, and a more serious difficulty, is that our daily experience of one another (and of nature) is that we are separate, distinct and different. It is difficult to believe that all that has to be done is to uncover, discover and read this essential unity at the heart of, and in the depths of, our experience – because life does not seem like that. For example, community is an ideal which is rightly a proper concern for churches – but it remains most elusive in practice. We say we want to establish a proper 'community' and we look for the opposite of fragmentation and competition. We seek comfort, not conflict, intimacy and warmth between persons, not distance. We yearn for affirmation, good will and collaboration instead of criticism. Yet community remains elusive.

I remain sceptical of those who affirm that it is only a matter of discovering our essential unity with one another and nature, with God within this world, that our hope lies. But what I have lately learnt from this mystical tradition is to begin to savour what Matthew Fox calls so wisely the Original Blessing of all creation and to recognize, celebrate and enjoy that the primary revelation of God is in nature.

The truth is that we are at odds with nature; we have been struggling too long with nature, and caused too much havoc, too much destruction to uncover some fundamental 'oneness' with everything. Precisely because there has been so much destruction, there is also the opportunity to recreate what has been lost. Rex Ambler puts it well:

> God is therefore mediated through the new possibilities that can inspire us to bring that about. God is ahead. God comes to us . . . out of the future, beckoning us to a new world, that we ourselves must help to create. God answers to our freedom and responsibility, . . . but also to our longing for unity and life, which binds us with all creatures. So God is the creative source of our life, that lures us into becoming what we have it in us to become.[6]

*   *   *

Thus it is from the voices at the margins, in appreciating the tradition of *chutzpah*, and in re-thinking and imagining our lives in relation to nature, that God discloses his or her self, lures us beyond what is known and familiar to build some steps towards a new future.

I said that the reason I left the Church was that everyday life was not valued. Much of what I have tried to describe adds up to that appreciation of the 'everyday' – particularly in affirming the dignity of men and women, and the struggles for that dignity to be recognized. Also and equally we can recognize and celebrate nature as that which, before all religious institutions, mediates God's intimate and amazing presence. If nature is honoured, if women and men are accorded the dignity due to them as made in the image of God, then in that honouring and the struggle for dignity is God.

I have been writing about the incarnation of God in the world; and only in as far as every person, and every living thing, has the capacity to reflect God, can I begin to speak of God revealed in Jesus Christ, else he is merely an alien, and an intruding stranger. Were I to write about the doctrine of the incarnation, it would begin from just that point.

NOTES

1 The hymn 'From Greenland's icy mountains', which was popular at Sherborne, is no longer included in modern hymn books, and rightly so. The imperialism and racist overtones are strange, coming from the innocent and saintly author, Reginald Heber (1783–1826), who wrote the hymn when he was Rector of Hadnet in Shropshire; he later became Bishop of Calcutta.

2 'We have lost some quality of experience which allows us to see the world as they did – or rather to see through it as they did. I take the animist world view to be just that: things were once transparent to the human eye; greater realities moved behind and within them, were seen in this or that, here and there as if through a lens': Theodore Roszak, *The Voice of the Earth* (New York: Simon & Schuster, 1992), p. 93.

3 Thomas Berry, *The Dream of the Earth* (San Francisco: Sierra Club Books, 1988), p. 123.

4 Brian Swimme and Thomas Berry, *The Universe Story* (San Francisco: Harper, 1992), p. 238.

5 *The Dream of the Earth*, ch. 7, 'Economics as a religious issue', p. 87.

6 Rex Ambler, 'Where on earth is God?' in Frances Young (ed.), *Dare We Speak of God In Public?* (London: Mowbray, 1995), p. 98.

3

Public and private

JUST BEFORE THE GULF WAR, the sermon at the Eucharist at St James's, Piccadilly was preached in an unusual manner. With the prospect of an invasion of Kuwait imminent in which Britain would be involved, I felt it was right for the congregation to 'create' the sermon together, using the rationale of the theory of the Just War.

The process of the sermon was more interesting than the outcome. The Sunday before, I announced that a more participatory type of address would take place, considering the question 'Would it be right to go to war against Saddam Hussein?' This notice invited everyone to do some preliminary thinking.

The sermon, which took place at the end of the liturgy, was in three sections. I spoke for ten minutes: the congregation, some 250, were then invited to talk to one another. There was then an opportunity to respond to what I had said, or as others spoke to respond to one another. Sometimes comments were addressed to me: invariably I passed them back to the congregation. This process was repeated twice: the 'sermon' lasted about fifty minutes. I did not attempt to summarize it or come to any conclusion. Everyone had the opportunity to speak. No one had to do so. The only ground rules I set were that we should respect each other's view and listen as carefully as we could to one another. There were more people who wanted to speak than there was time: there were strong differences expressed. There was laughter, anger and silence.

What was disconcerting about that 'sermon' (a process which I have used sparingly when controversial issues are being considered) was the reaction of relief and gratitude – out of all proportion to the event itself. It has taken me some time to realize that there are few places, few occasions, few talking shops where the public can gather and in a welcoming and safe place test out their thoughts, opinions and ideas.

The congregation on that Sunday, just before the Gulf War, consisted of a small group of those who knew one another well, a larger group who knew each other less well, and, being a city-centre church in London, a considerable number of visitors from different parts of the world. In the private world of the family, views remain unchecked and unthought-out because they are familiar to everyone. During that sermon there was a process of education by which members of the public educated themselves and each other. Strangers, acquaintances, and friends met on common ground. In our private lives, strangers do not intrude, for they are not welcome. In public life, in that varied congregation in the middle of London on a wet January Sunday morning, I was reminded (though not till later, as I reflected about the sermon) that the foundation of our life together is not just the intimate and private circle of family and friends, but the interaction and capacity of us all to share common problems, common resources, because the whole human race and the earth are inter-dependent and inter-related. Our interdependence is a given fact of life, and in honouring the stranger as part and parcel of the fabric of our lives together, it is not necessary for strangers to become friends.

Our public life affirms that we are all members, one of another, all inter-dependent whether we like it or not. That is the way the world is, and this recognition is, or should be, at the heart of religion. The word 'religion' comes from the Latin word to bind together or to rebind. The stories which Jesus told arise from his longing that all should be included in the Kingdom of God – not least those whom the world rejects. Thus, too, among some Christian communities there is a passionate and abiding concern for justice, so that the reconciliation, when it happens, restores those links which had been broken. Such a fundamental perception of religion also colours the practice of a few wealthy people who believe quite simply that their wealth is to be shared, and that it is a privilege to do so.

The sense of the 'public' has disintegrated in our culture. When this happens, politics becomes either a theatre of illusion or a dangerous side-show, because there are few flourishing voluntary associations to check the inevitable thrust towards oppression, to which unchecked power points. Instead we live at a time when the private is idealized; many aspects of our lives have been privatized – not least our religion. We are addressed as citizens, customers, and consumers – our identity is defined in totally indi-vidualistic ways. This is inevitable given the competition of the unfettered market, which has poisoned the substance of our community life, as the gap between rich and poor grows year by year. In the absence of any consensus, any sense of our common life together, or of the common good, the tawdry demands of the market prevail.

It is widely believed that closeness between persons is the primary moral good: we aspire to develop close, warm, trusting relationships. This can become an ideology or tyranny of intimacy: 'warmth' is our God. This means that the public, the mass of people 'out there' are experienced as a threatening presence, or as a backdrop to working out our own problems. As far as possible the 'public' are to be avoided.

Churches and some forms of therapy sometimes endorse this tyranny of intimacy. Even congregations which pride themselves on being open are skilful in squeezing out those who do not fit. I know of flourishing suburban Anglican churches, very much churches for the family, where gay men, known to be gay and happy to be so, soon discover they are not welcome. The most 'open' and 'welcoming' of churches create their own identity at the expense of minorities they exclude. So often churches give the impression of being communities in retreat; as the language of psychobabble puts it: 'Churches are places you dump all your emotional baggage: they are used for emotional expressions of relief.'

When this happens, people are disabled. Conflicts are concealed or denied, and opportunities to face up to them, to resolve them and turn to change, do not happen. It is then an easy step to put down the causes of all society's problems and difficulties to alienation or to coldness between people. In such diseased and unhealthy congregations no amount of preaching about structural sin – the way that we organize ourselves which perpetuates injustice and inequality – makes the slightest difference.

Some forms of therapy contribute to this enfeebling of the 'public'. It is symptomatic of the ways in which the sense of community, of belonging, has been so weakened, that when a traumatic event happens, a man going berserk with a gun, killing and maiming, professional counsellors have to be drafted in. Given the disappearance of community, neighbourliness, the art of listening, friendship, and tapping into the wisdom and experience of the elderly and the disappearance of local government, it is not surprising, but what a reflection on our 'public life' together or lack of it.

There is, of course, a place for counselling. As I said, I have profited from it, but it has now developed into a middle-class industry which reinforces the poverty of our 'public life', for invariably counselling aims to help a person stand on her own feet, so that she becomes independent and autonomous. In the probing and exploration of her relationships, her feelings and her attitudes, only the self remains. Any hint, say, of self-sacrifice and giving away of her life for others is too easily regarded as a diversion and in the way of discovering the true self. I have noticed that dependence on a counsellor, which is a customary part of the healing process, may create a lack of will to rebuild links with others.

What I am trying to say is that each of us has to wake up (and stay awake) to what is happening on the planet and in our own lives, and then in a multitude of ways begin to make choices which will start off the process of sustainable revolution.[1] Inevitably this will be bumpy, dangerous and uncertain. If a living process of celebrating the public can be established and experienced now, then we will help one another to come out of the shadows and take our part. The Gulf War sermon was a modest example of such a process, and the tangible sense of relief, expressed then for that opportunity to explore, share and debate an important matter, showed both the paucity of the experience of the 'public' and the need for such a process.

*   *   *

In *The Company of Strangers*, Parker J. Palmer quotes a cab driver as he careered up Broadway:

> You get to know the public. Which teaches you a lot in life. You don't know anything if you don't know the public. You exchange ideas and you learn a lot from people. It's like going to school. Meeting all these different kinds of people, everything helps, it doesn't hurt. If you only like one kind of people, it's no good! We talk, if I have a better idea I tell them. Maybe they say yes, maybe they say no – that's how I educate myself. It makes me happy. You can't buy this kind of education. If you're with the same kind of people all the time, it's like wearing the same suit all the time – you get sick of it. But the public – that keeps you alive.[2]

The cab driver's words are a celebration of the 'public' – what needs to happen so that this perception of the public can be experienced?

There is a need to recover the true meaning and practice of hospitality. Hospitality has degenerated into a harmless urbane quality associated with 'entertaining'; it is associated with exhausting small talk, civility and amiable politeness. But Henri Nouwen, the Roman Catholic writer, sees hospitality differently:

> Ancient hospitality is firstly and primarily a bond between utter strangers . . . the paradox of hospitality is that it wants to create an

emptiness, not a fearful emptiness, but a friendly emptiness where strangers can enter and discover themselves as created free, free to sing their own songs, speak their own languages, dance their own dances; free also to leave and follow their own vocations. Hospitality is not a subtle invitation to adopt the lifestyle of the host, but the gift of a chance for the guest to find his own.[3]

This is much easier said than done. My exhortations ring hollow in the face of our society, which for many generations has been deeply flawed by racism. This is embedded in our culture in a sense of the inferior status of the foreigner, as if he lacked something and is quite different from us. Kipling expresses this with his typically crude eloquence:

> The stranger within my gate,
> He may be true or kind,
> But he does not talk my talk,
> I cannot feel his mind.
> I see the face and the eyes and mouth
> But not the soul behind.

Western European Christianity developed these attitudes: emerging out of the imperial worlds of Greece and Rome, Christians have presented themselves to those of other faiths as effortlessly superior. That is deeply offensive to Jews, Muslims, Hindus and Buddhists. Imperial attitudes do not sit easily in a society where brothers and sisters of our religious traditions wish to enjoy their own religious and cultural inheritance.

Moreover, once a 'foreigner' has been allowed entry to stay as a resident, the English have required that he is absorbed and assimilated into our culture, so as far as possible he becomes like one of us. A classic example are the Huguenots, some of whom settled in England but of whom today there is absolutely no trace except for a few buildings and surnames.

Rabbi Tony Bayfield, in his Cardinal Bea Memorial Lecture of 1993, quotes a celebrated example of this attitude to the stranger in an interview given by Norman Tebbit in April 1990. Mr Tebbit was then Conservative Party Chairman; he used the example of a cricket Test Match, and suggested that the Asian community were not supporting the right side. 'Which side do they cheer for?' he asked. 'It's an interesting test. Are you still harking back to where you came from or where you are? I think we have got real problems in that regard.' In other words, in return for acceptance into British society, the Asians should renounce their history, their culture, their loyalty to their own roots and identify with Alan Lamb rather than Waqar

Younis. And this comes very oddly from a citizen of that Empire which littered the countries they ruled with their racially segregated clubs, excluding anyone whose skin wasn't white.

It is not for me (as an Anglican and an Englishman) to say how minority communities relate to a dominant culture – the extent to which they choose to remain separate or become absorbed. But they must be free to choose. The implications of the words of Norman Tebbit, and those who think like him, have to be continually resisted.

Practising hospitality means vigilance for and on behalf of the stranger – and all the evidence points to practices which are inhospitable. Levels of discrimination and disadvantage remain alarmingly high even though it is now more than fifteen years since the Race Relations Act was passed. Ethnic minorities have a 60 per cent higher unemployment rate than white people. They experience discrimination in the allocation of housing, health education and welfare benefits. They experience often terrifying levels of harassment, abuse and physical violence. The police, time and again, fail to provide protection for the victims of racial violence.

There is, however, one particular difficulty which confronts Christianity in its relationships to minorities and other faiths. It is that of evangelism. To seek to change the faith of someone else is fraught with difficulties. Christian hospitality affirms that communities, other than Christian, have a right to exist in our country, and they should be free to follow their own beliefs and cultures. Part of our responsibility is to ensure that such communities are protected from racist threats and attacks over which they are often powerless.

How then can the gospel be shared or proposed to those of other faiths? It is impossible to answer such a question satisfactorily. To avoid it raises further questions about the nature of faith, and the convictions it generates. If this is the truth for me, then it has to be the truth for all, yet prior to that certainty there is the more fundamental responsibility of welcoming communities of other faiths.

Perhaps an answer begins to emerge in the context of a long-term perspective. To stand in the presence of the stranger whose religion is different from our own is to move into uncharted territory. It is to become aware of standing on a threshold as the 'otherness' of the stranger becomes apparent. It is only too easy for us, as the 'host' country, to doubt, disbelieve or dismiss the experience of people of other colours and creeds; and it is only too easy to keep power and control in our own hands in relation to the stranger. Before the welcoming and the talking there is the listening to the mystery of the Other revealed in the stranger's presence. Our hospitality requires at least this attention so that friends and strangers together may cross the threshold into paths none of us can foresee.[4]

Such levels of injustice and inhumanity are highly pertinent to the sustainable and environmental revolution, which is on the way, and the outcome of which depends, as I have said, on so many different choices. Thus if limitless and unrestricted growth is to be checked, there will be scapegoats to blame for what will inevitably mean a lower standard of living for everyone. Unless we are vigilant, minorities of every sort will be the first to suffer. Therefore, as a matter of urgency, ways and means have to be found in which the strangers, the immigrants, are not forced to abandon their own roots, but are allowed to find their own way.

Meanwhile, the Church of England, unlike many organizations, and unlike other denominations, is well placed to practise this vigilance and insist on recognizing and welcoming the diversity of our communities, since through the system of geographical parishes (which remains just about intact) it is present in the most neglected and deprived areas. And one of the ways in which churches, together with many other organizations, can remain vigilant and consider all the issues around the stranger, is to bring people together to discuss them, to create alternative forums where there may be proper listening and informed and tough debate.

There is plenty of disagreement in our society and within the churches, but little debate. By debate I mean a passionate struggle with one another to discover the truth which can never be mastered. It means listening and learning from the arguments of opponents, trying to discover what is right, what they affirm, before their arguments are found wanting.

No one, no organization, possesses the truth; the truth belongs to God alone. As John Donne put it, 'On a huge hill, cragged and steep, Truth stands, and he that will reach her about must, and about must go'. I have been inspired by the witness of the churches in Eastern Germany before the Revolution. The great churches of Dresden and Leipzig were the places where public debate on public matters took place. They provided the cradle for the Revolution. It was the example of such churches in the 1980s which led St James's, Piccadilly, to offer a modest, alternative forum where matters of public interest and public concern can be publicly debated. In the light of the way in which the 'right' has hijacked so much of our language – about freedom and democracy, for example – the creation of such forums is the very least that can be done.

Debate implies a humility before truth, a courtesy towards the other person, and a reverence for words. Since as strangers and friends we share a common humanity, we belong together and can talk together. Words are precious; and need to be used carefully, thoughtfully, and with respect. When society disintegrates, words are treated with contempt.

Timothy Radcliffe, in a talk given at *The Tablet*'s Open Day in June

1994, gives a graphic account of his experiences of the power of words and the hatred they provoke. He says that when he was in San Salvador he went

> to visit the rooms where the Jesuits were gunned down in the university. The murderers also shot their books. You can see a copy of Kittel's *Theological Dictionary of the New Testament*, open at the page on the Holy Spirit, source of all wisdom, ripped across into bullet holes. I think of the library of a priest in Haiti, books all destroyed and torn up: I think of a little village on the border of Croatia and Serbia, shelled out of existence, with the very bodies from the graves dug up and thrown around, and the missal in the church torn and desecrated with obscenities.[5]

*　　*　　*

I have tried to show the sense of the 'public' needs to be reclaimed, and what is involved in establishing a process by which 'public life' – our life together – is experienced. I have illustrated this most obviously and appropriately in a consideration of 'hospitality' and the place of the stranger in church and society.

We are starved of opportunities of public debate; when this happens well, solidarity and celebration are experienced. These occasions are not just talking shops. Some years ago I invited Matthew Fox and Dorothee Sölle to a public dialogue on 'Is there hope for the First World?' Matthew Fox, an American and former Dominican, is a theologian, teacher and writer about creation spirituality. Dorothee Sölle, a German, is a radical feminist theologian, active all her life in peace and liberation movements. She is one of the heroes of the Left in post-war Germany. Both have been in trouble with their churches. Both disagreed with each other fundamentally on many issues. Three hundred people came to listen and to join in. They were of all ages and religions. After two and a half hours I felt it was right to bring the evening to an end. After all, the seats were hard and people had to get home. There were strong protests – 'Why can't we go on all night?' someone said, and there was a strong murmur of approval.

Even though the two speakers disagreed, they respected one another (and I think they liked one another). Their dialogue drew out testimonies, comments and questions from the audience of as a high a quality as the dialogue itself. Everyone was reluctant to leave. Amid the arguments, the anger, the laughter, the struggle and the silences there was solidarity and celebration, or as I would want to put it, an experience of public life transformed by God's promise of reconciliation and hope for us all.

NOTES

1 See p. 22, note 7.

2 Parker J. Palmer, *The Company of Strangers – Christians and the Renewal of America's Public Life* (New York: Crossroad, 1986) – an inspiration for this chapter.

3 Henri Nouwen, *Reaching Out* (Garden City, NY: Doubleday, 1975), p. 51.

4 There is a stream of theologians who have influenced me in the consideration of the Other: Martin Buber, John Robinson, Walter Brueggemann, and particularly the philosopher Emmanuel Levinas in *Time and the Other*, reproduced in *A Levinas Reader*, edited by Sean Hand (Oxford: Basil Blackwell, 1989), p. 37. An introduction to Levinas' thinking can be found in Michael Barnes SJ, 'Evangelisation – the Other: response and responsibility', *The Month* (December 1992).

5 Timothy Radcliffe OP, 'Jurassic Park or Last Supper?', *The Tablet* (18 June 1994).

CHAPTER

4

Leaders

IN FEBRUARY 1988 Dr John Habgood, then Archbishop of York, made a sensible proposal in a radio interview that couples about to be married should be eligible for tax concessions and housing benefits. Shortly afterwards, I was invited to take part in a 60-minute phone-in programme on Air UK to respond to callers about the Archbishop's comments. While there were some who addressed directly the Archbishop's ideas, most did not. The general response was 'Here's the old C of E again up to its tricks – the Archbishop wants to prop it up by bribing people to come to church'.

This was certainly not what the Archbishop said, or even implied. What came across from most callers was the cynicism they had about leaders. Political leaders were in politics for power, and what money they could make on the side. Church leaders, like the Archbishop in this case, were thought to be acting entirely in their own interest. The lack of a public life, which I have already referred to, and the notion of public service which has almost vanished has led to a mistrust of leadership. Yet never has there been a time when wisdom and discernment are needed among leaders – among world leaders, politicians, religious and community leaders, and leaders (if that word can be used) of families.

I have been inspired by some words of Vaclav Havel, former playwright, dissident, prisoner and now President of the Czech Republic. Speaking to the US Congress in 1990 he reminded them of how much his country suffered under the Soviet Union; he spoke of 'a legacy of countless dead, an infinite spectrum of human suffering, profound economic decline and above all enormous human humiliation'. He then goes on:

It has given us something positive, a special capacity to look from time to time somewhat further than someone who has not undergone this bitter experience. A person who cannot move and live a somewhat normal life because he is pinned under a boulder has more time to think about his hopes than someone who is not trapped that way.

And then he says

We too can offer something to you: our experience and the knowledge that has come from it. The specific experience I am talking about has given me one certainty: consciousness precedes being, and not the other way round, as the Marxists claim.

(He could also have included capitalists but given the audience was probably too polite to do so.)

For this reason the salvation of this human world lies nowhere else than in the human heart, in the human power to reflect, in human meekness and in human responsibility. Without a global revolution in the sphere of human consciousness nothing will change for the better in the sphere of our being as humans, and the catastrophe towards which this world is headed . . . will be unavoidable.[1]

President Havel's words are echoed in all religious traditions: what is fundamental, and the true source of all power and freedom lies in the human heart. It is not the world of 'matter' but that of spirit, consciousness, human awareness, the imagination. Here is found the hope of the oppressed, the capacity to wrestle with God, and the sense of our connectedness with one another and the earth (as we saw in Chapter 2) We live through a complex movement between what is inside of us – the inner life – and what is 'out there'. We create the world and make it what it is by projecting our spirit – whether of despair or hope, darkness, greyness or light – on to what is 'out there'.

Leaders are those who have power over, or influence over, others and cast either dark shadows or light about them. Thus a leader needs to take responsibility for what is going on inside him- or herself, or their leadership does more harm than good. By leaders, I am thinking of anyone who is in a 'power over' position – he or she may also be a decision-maker, a consultant, an opinion-former, a social worker, teacher, chief executive, assistant manager in a store, as well as a politician either in power or one who seeks power.

What I have noticed is that those in positions of power often deny the inner consciousness to which President Havel draws our attention. So, for example, I have met politicians who regard this inner world as a fantasy or waste of time – an invention of the clergy, perhaps a topic for a few moments at the weekend, but otherwise to be ignored, so confident are they of themselves in managing the external world around them in the pursuit of their own interests. The inner life is screened out. But it cannot ultimately be ignored, because to do so is to cause a lot of damage among those whom leaders operate, and over whom they have power or influence.

The inner life has been described by Annie Dillard like this:

In the deeps are the violence and terror of which psychology has warned us. But if you ride these monsters deeper down, if you drop with them farther over the world's rim, you find what our sciences cannot locate or name, the substrata, the ocean or matrix or ether which buries the rest, which gives goodness its power for good, and evil its power for evil, the unified field: our complex and inexplicable caring for each other, and for our life together here. This is given, it is not learned.[2]

The best leaders are those who make and continue to make that journey. That is why Nelson Mandela is a great leader. After 30 years of prison, he emerged not cynical, bitter or despairing, not concerned for his own fame or fortune, not driven by a lust for power, but as one who strives to lead all his people to that 'place' where there is true community.

The process of the inner journey is neither therapy nor morbid introspection. What starts the journey off may be some interruption of life which has been taken for granted: the break-up of a marriage, or imprisonment, or being made redundant. It is a process of attention and reflection not just to what is happening 'out there', but also 'inside'. This inner work is personal, but not necessarily private; it could happen within a group of trusted friends who meet for this exploration regularly and as a natural part of living.

I have noticed in myself as a parish priest and also in others what happens when the inner life is ignored, and the work on the soul ceases. Many leaders appear to have a deep insecurity about their own worth; they are in constant need of affirmation, and often do everything they can to create settings which deprive others of their identity as a way of dealing with unexamined fears in themselves. An elderly and now retired bishop told me that when he was consecrated he enjoyed wearing his mitre, pectoral cross and episcopal ring; he enjoyed carrying his pastoral staff, thumping the floor with it as he processed up the aisle. He said that now 'I realize I relished that because I was not sure of myself; but I wonder what my behaviour did to other people, to the congregations to which I had been invited'. Did it encourage or discourage them? 'I think I know the answer', he said. 'Now I would just like to slip into my place.'

When I meet wise doctors and wise nurses, they often say 'You don't know what we do sometimes to the patients – how we deprive them of their identity to give ourselves more status and more importance'.

But then I heard another bishop talking at a luncheon to 60 businessmen and women. He was speaking about his job, about what he does, and what he feels about it. His audience was clearly impressed by the bishop's capacity for hard work. And then he said 'I begin each day with prayer, because at the end of the day I am only David Hope' (it was the then Bishop of London who was speaking) 'and this day may be my last'.

What the bishop was implying was that he realized that titles, degrees, fancy robes, and the power he has, matter less than his awareness that he, like everyone else, is a child of God. And to recognize that, although the bishop did not say this, is to call into question patriarchy (which says that men are superior to women and that men can dominate nature), and hierarchy (where authority is exercised from on high).

I have noticed in myself and in others that the universe is seen as essentially hostile; that we live in a competitive world which is really a scene of a vast combat. Such prophecy is self-fulfilling. In central London I know how. Worried chief executives talk about the competitive world; how they are going to survive, how the banks are closing in. The language and practice of competition is now so part of our everyday reality that it takes some insight to recognize that there is another way of perceiving the world – that the universe is not out to get anybody, and that to take the journey downwards is to discover our solidarity with each other.

With the pressures of individualism and competition belong a functional atheism, particularly noticeable in the clergy. The functional atheist believes that 'ultimate responsibility rests with me. No decent thing is going to happen in this place, unless I make it happen.' That is why some clergy suffer from burn-out, become workaholics, and have unrealistic priorities. They become simply boring and unbearable as people. To take the inner journey is to realize that ours is not the only act in town, that we can share and trust others to collaborate.

It is certainly difficult, as I well know, for a leader to admit that he makes mistakes. Because our culture is so addicted to 'success', it cannot easily tolerate leaders who, through lack of judgement or whatever, admit to making mistakes. It is one of the most common complaints about politicians that they will not admit that what they did was wrong, rather they insist that what they are doing they have always done, and it is only a matter of time, and the recession will end, the economy will recover and all will be well. But we are not fooled. As scientists know well, every mistake, every failure, is an opportunity for learning, and to lead on to a new development. It has to be possible to create a new culture in which leaders have opportunities to learn, admit uncertainty and acknowledge mistakes.

Part of this learning is the recognition of the creativity of chaos. Leaders who are just managers do everything they can to eliminate dissent, change and innovation. What they fail to realize is that hope and vitality only emerge out of chaos, as the archetypal movement of the human spirit is one of death and resurrection. In the same way, the best leaders will recognize how much of institutional life is dead. So many parts of our institutions – in the church, or the monarchy, for example – seem to have been on a life-support system for years: death of institutions, the dying of us all, is a natural and welcome part of life, not something to be ignored or covered up.

It is appropriate at this point to consider the leaders whom I know best, and they are the bishops of the Church of England. One of the reasons for a crisis in leadership is the way leadership and management have become confused. Much care is now taken in the selection and training of men and women for the ordained ministry; continuing training, job appraisals, pastoral care of the clergy – all these are becoming commonplace and more professional. The clergy, including bishops and senior church leaders, have probably never been so competent, hard-working, moderate – and dull. But competence, diligence and moderation are not enough to commend membership of a church – all the main line denominations are in decline. Organized religion is regarded by the majority as pointless; it is becoming expensive to be a member, not least with the upkeep of buildings, and time-consuming as well – with the plethora of committees and meetings which church membership now entails.

What has happened is that the clergy have become managers; we are maintenance men and women holding our communities together. Declining organizations spawn paper work, and all sorts of devices to keep them going. Managing is reactive. Management is about control. Management ensures smooth running on a day-to-day basis with budgets and financial planning. Management, as someone has said, is doing things right; leadership is doing the right thing.

The leader as manager was brought home to me in the 1980s when the Urban Ministry Project (of which I was a director) and the William Temple

Foundation arranged two in-service training programmes for bishops and senior church leaders. They identified tensions in their ministries, expressed in our report like this:

Chosen and set apart for leadership	yet	seeking at every point to share that leaderhip with others
A guardian of the faith and practice of the Church	yet	an interpreter of that faith and practice in new ways
A manager and decision maker	yet	an enabler and encourager of others to make their own decisions
A focus of unity	yet	a promoter of a variety of styles of being the Church which are appropriate in some, but not all, circumstances
An administrator of discipline	yet	a caring, sympathetic and forgiving pastor

The report goes on: 'It was recognised that perhaps the fundamental experience of leadership in the contemporary Church lies precisely in having to live in and through these and other tensions.'[3]

These tensions are recognizable in many jobs; what is required of this type of leader is patience, tact, clarity and the ability to hold together that part of the institution over which he or she is in charge. Consultation, collaboration and co-operation are characteristic activities.

But while the institution may hold together it will inevitably be timid in what it says and does, because its leaders will want to minimize conflicts and invariably, given human nature and the drive to protect their own interests, will seek to enhance its standing with the powerful. Thus, for example, everyone in the British churches condemns racism (although there is some evidence that there are concentrations of racism, anti-Semitism and homophobia in the churches), but when practical implications are involved, like contributing to a special programme to combat racism, or campaigning against an immigration bill, or taking part in a demonstration against the British National Party, Christians draw back in large numbers. We pray for peace and speak of justice as long as it costs nothing. This is what I mean by timidity, and it is absolutely irresistible as long as the leader is experienced as a manager.

So many of us parish priests and bishops have become more like chief executives of a shrinking business than spiritual leaders. But the Church deserves something better. The Church of England is being presented with an opportunity to refound itself within the next quarter of a century. But it will not happen through management.

What has brought this opportunity is the financial mess of the Church of England, which has been with us for over fifty years and exacerbated by the losses incurred by the Church Commissioners in 1993. By the end of the century the salaries of all the clergy will have to be found from the quota levied by dioceses on parishes. Already many parishes are defaulting. Churches with small congregations feel guilty that they cannot pay their share; they worry whether when their priest leaves there will be a successor, or whether they will be tacked on to another parish. As the quota contribution increases, and the congregations fall because of the death of more elderly members, they will have no choice but to default. The energies of more and more churches will become consumed with fundraising in order to just exist. Evangelical parishes, who are among the biggest contributors to the diocese via the quota, threaten to withhold their payments in the light of what they see as the liberalizing of the church. Some wealthier congregations resent having to make up what others cannot pay. Sometimes there is considerable mistrust of bishops and 'the diocese'. It is not inconceivable, given the sudden collapse of business, that a diocese could face bankruptcy. The clergy could no longer be paid. The apprehension and anxiety of this situation certainly inhibit anyone who might be interested in Christianity from joining.

There is, however, another way which draws on some of the insights which I described as the 'inner life' of leaders. The bishops could say to their people: 'We recognize that the way the finances of the Church of England operate is crippling our parishes: we believe that sooner or later this structure will collapse. We believe that we should let this happen now. We ask you to pay your priest's salary. There will be two years for you to make the necessary arrangements. You will not have to contribute anything to central funds. We recognize that this is the end of much of the bureaucracy you associate with the diocese and with me. But we trust you. We wish to empower you to take charge of your own affairs. We know that within every congregation and from among those who might wish to join there is much talent; the potential in all of you for ministry is astonishing and has yet to be realized. We recognize that what we are saying will initiate a period of much confusion and pain; some parishes will require their priest to find part-time work; others will dispense with paid clergy altogether. But in anticipating this collapse, we believe there are opportunities for vitality to blossom. We already know of such flourishing communities.

'For ourselves, we shall be free of much of the administration and elaborate organizations of the diocese; we will do everything we can to assist in developing partnerships between richer and poorer parishes in the Church of England and between churches in the developing world from whom we have much to learn – remembering St Paul's advice that we should bear one another's burdens for that is the law of Christ. We will then be free to visit you, to learn from you, and to share with you the riches of the Christian tradition. When we come to your communities we do not wish to be greeted with great ceremony. All we ask is for a chair to be placed in some central space. Then we will invite any who will to gather round so that together we can speak of what God is requiring of us all in these difficult and threatening times – then we will pray and celebrate the Eucharist.'

There are risks in this approach. One is the possibility of the break-up of the Church of England. One of the alarming aspects of the Church is how its different parts – Catholic, Liberal and Protestant (each with their own divisions) – now exist independently of each other. This is not the comprehensive Church of England I grew up in, where there was a recognizable holding together of its different parts. At its worst it looks more like a conglomeration of congregations. Another risk is the prospect of a takeover of the Church by various Protestant groups. Another is the turmoil which will have to be dealt with in every parish.

But the advantages are greater. If the financial arrangements of the Church are not and will not be working, then it is best to acknowledge the facts, and anticipate the situation. Then the fear of the infiltration of the Church of England by different brands of Evangelicals is real, but only up to a point. English spirituality is moderate (or phlegmatic!), practical, domestic and lay – that is our cultural inheritance. We mistrust fanaticism or 'enthusiasm', as it was known in the eighteenth century. Furthermore, there is evidence of a considerable number of young people moving away from a narrow Evangelical base to a broader perspective.[4] And in the light of what I said in Chapter 1 on the methodology of liberation theology there emerges the possibility of the growth of a vibrant lay movement within the Church.

The ramifications of my imaginary bishops' statement (and I doubt if they would ever agree to speak with one voice on this matter) are considerable, and well beyond the scope of this book, which is not about the structure of the Church of England. And I am not writing about structures or strategies, or aims and objectives, but about a fundamental prompting of the human spirit. We preach about death and resurrection; perhaps all of us, particularly our leaders, may have to be prepared to let go our structures and our financial arrangements, and trust the people.

NOTES

1 Speech by Vaclav Havel, quoted in Parker J. Palmer, *Leading from Within – Reflections on Spirituality and Leadership* (The Servant Leadership School, 1640 Columbia Road NW, Washington, DC 20009).
2 Annie Dillard, *Teaching a Stone to Talk*, quoted in *Leading from Within*.
3 Report on in-service training for bishops and senior Church leaders arranged by the Urban Ministry Project and the William Temple Foundation (1984).
4 A well-known post-Evangelical Christian community is the 'Nine O'Clock Service' in Sheffield.

5

Down in the world

THE PICTURE OF THE 'IDEAL' LEADER which begins to emerge from what I have written is far removed from the popular perception of the contemporary leader – powerful, virile (whether man or woman), rugged, undaunted by circumstances, and always right. Leaders learn about the inner life through the wisdom of religions, through prayer, and the study of sacred scriptures. But more needs to be said about this 'learning process', in the light of what I have written about our connectedness one with another and our solidarity with each other.

Amongst the extensive literature on leadership, on positive learning, time management, aims and objectives, I have never come across anything about how the human heart is 'educated'. I believe our teachers in this education, as well as the traditional wisdom and the process of inner work, are those of whom we are frightened, reject and ignore – namely the poor.

It is in this context that I will consider our attitude to the mentally ill who are also homeless.

It is difficult for those who are not mentally ill to imagine what it must be like to be so. It is even more difficult to imagine what it must be like to be homeless and mentally ill, with brains not functioning properly. They live like rats, living off leftovers. They trust nobody. They are invariably scorned by other members of the homeless community.

When I think of the mentally ill who are homeless I think of them as the afflicted ones. Simone Weil describes them as if they had been struck by blows that leave a human being struggling on the ground like a half-crushed worm. The afflicted ones: these are the ones we cannot bear to look at, the ones we keep away from because they smell, the ones we would never think of taking in our arms. The mentally ill have always been feared and have always been badly treated. Michel Foucault, the French philosopher, describes how in the Middle Ages the mentally ill were put on to ships. They sailed up and down the rivers and canals. When they arrived at the quayside or at the port everyone would come out and laugh at them. Our history is full of accounts of the homeless mentally ill, usually foraging in villages, living like animals.

In the seventeenth and eighteenth centuries they began to confine them in large institutions – places like Bedlam which would certainly make a wise man mad, rather than a mad man wise. Little has changed in our attitudes to the homeless and the mentally ill, in spite of all our civilized ways: I find myself not wanting to look into the faces of the crazy. I am both frightened and I am also frightened of being rejected. It is strange that I, who am so secure, should fear the rejection of a deranged person.

Nothing will change for the homeless, nor for the mentally ill who are homeless, unless the public is given a new heart. Our failure is in not allowing what we see and hear every day to sink into our hearts. We have to educate our emotions, and that needs to be a priority for leaders. We have campaigns and that is right; we have attempts to do community care, and all that is right. But we hear little about the failure of us all to educate our sensibilities, our emotions and our feelings towards the mentally ill.

Why do we turn away from the afflicted, why do I turn away from them as they wander about central London? We need to name the reasons why we turn away from them so we can disarm our hearts and learn from them. And if we can understand our reasons this may help in the development of a mature emotional response, and in the nurture of wise leaders.

The first reason why we turn away from them is that affliction is anonymous; it deprives its victims of their personalities and makes them into things: we just do not see bundles of rags as human beings engaged in the struggle to survive.

The greater the affliction the more we are repulsed. I therefore need to know the extent of the abysmal suffering of those who are mentally ill. We are often completely unaware of our ambivalence. I think many clergy and those who are in the 'caring professions', and people who are Christian and conscious of being so, are particularly unaware of their ambivalence to the afflicted. We are probably too attached to ourselves as 'caring persons' to admit we are repelled. After all, we are supposed to love everybody, we are supposed to care, but we do not actually admit the fact that we want to put these people always out to sea. We are not as removed from the Middle Ages as we think.

Furthermore, the homeless mentally ill are disturbing because we do not think they have feelings like the rest of us. We cannot grasp the dreadful emptiness of those who have ceased to talk to us and can only talk to themselves. This destructive, 'antisocial' behaviour is due to bewilderment, to mistreatment, to fright and depression. It is hard to understand what it is like to have a mind in such disarray; they cannot tell us how their world feels. So we have to use the imagination. For us, eating is a pleasure, for the mentally ill, foraging in the dustbins means survival. For us, one aching tooth is quite enough to send us straight to the dentist; but many homeless people, and among them the mentally ill, often have mouths full of broken, decaying teeth.

Then we have to recognize one of the reasons we find it so hard to disarm our hearts is simply because society puts most of its resources at the disposal of those who are clean, educated and affluent. Many social workers and therapists prefer to work with the acceptable face of suffering than for those whom I have been describing. The well-to-do, educated sufferers will find much more access to all sorts of care than the people I am writing about. The garden of St James's, Piccadilly, sometimes offers sanctuary to some dozen or so alcoholic men in their fifties. Someone said to me 'What a pity some of the young homeless don't come into the garden. We could do something for them!'

It is difficult to explain the presence of a homeless population amidst our affluence. I get irritated with people who keep on talking about the lack of resources, when there are so many willing people who are unemployed. 'Resources' is a new word; twenty years ago we never used it. The problem, or the question, is why are we not angry about this situation? The lack of anger is galling. And what we have failed to notice is how large a price each of us pays in our self-esteem for not being connected with our enormous capacity to care: another lesson for leaders.

And, lastly, the most important reason of all is that in many of us there is a homeless person, a person that we keep out of sight and hearing. In many of us there is also a person who is not acceptable, whose own problem might cause us to be rejected. We project on to the mentally ill people on our streets our smaller problems: we then do not have to explore the disease in ourselves, we can keep in place these camps of 'we the caring people here' and 'them' out there. We may succeed even in keeping our illness secret, or in denying our illness and disease altogether.

Thus, to return to the education of the inner life of leaders, we have to practise consciously an awareness of our emotions: we have to get inside those dark dimensions and receive them into our consciousness: we have to look at these feelings of being repelled and allow ourselves to be transformed.

It is hard work and it is a continuing process. We have to learn how to forgive ourselves and to forgive one another for being less than we thought we were and less than we might be.

What I have described is the education of emotion, sensibility and feeling; it leads to the disarming of hearts. The teachers in this school for living and learning are not just books or religion, but the despairing, broken, angry faces of those whose minds have gone and have nowhere to rest.

As I have already said, in 1969 I attended a course in urban ministry at the Urban Training Centre in Chicago. To mark the transition from a busy, administrative job (a bishop's chaplain) to becoming a parish priest in south London, I went to Chicago. The purpose of the training was to turn clergy into community activists and organizers. The course began with the Plunge. We were given two dollars, and told to return in five days. There were no other instructions. We were invited to consider the experience on a retreat. On our return we had an extensive debriefing session – 'de-plunging' as it was called. It would have been easy enough to remain stuck with a whole range of entrenched stereotypes about poverty unless there was time to explore our experiences in some depth. Those few days began a process, which is still going on for me, of learning out of the life of the streets.

A novel which made a strong impression on me when it was first published in 1973 is Morris West's *The Shoes of the Fisherman*. It is the story of the first Slav Pope – Kiril, who before his election had been a prisoner in a Soviet jail for 17 years. In his journal, just after his election as Pope, he writes:

> The rumour of the city still reaches me on the night wind – footsteps, sounding hollow on stones, scream of motor tyres, the bleat of a horn, snatches of faraway song, and the slow clip of a tired horse . . . I want to walk out through the Angelic Gate and find my people where they stroll or sit together in the alleys of Trastevere . . . I need them so much more than they need me.[1]

And alone after his coronation, imprisoned in the Vatican as if in a fortress, he remembers stories of his childhood; how the Caliph Haroun disguised himself and walked out with his vizier to search the hearts of his people.

> I remember how Jesus the Master sat at meat with tax gatherers and public women, and I wonder why his successors were so eager to assume the penalty of princes, which is to rule from a secret room and to display oneself like a demi-god, only on occasions of public festivity.[2]

The Pope takes off his white soutane, and slips out of a back door of the Vatican dressed like an ordinary Catholic priest, and goes out into the streets of Rome.

When this process happens, leaders change. A bishop, for example, begins to learn from those whose place in society and experience is different from his own. Leaders who are continually flattered begin to believe they are where they are through their own merit; but they may realize that they arrive in their position invariably through chance, not choice. Leaders, particularly those with wealth, often believe they are morally superior and intellectually more capable than anyone else. Their new education should soon disabuse them.

A bishop or a priest who wishes to educate himself in the way I am describing will begin to develop a capacity for self-criticism. He will have come down in the world, and thus live closer to the truths of people's lives. His leadership will be marked by an attentive silence and serious listening, and when he is with his own kind, and only then, to pester, criticize and speak out. This style of leadership is particularly critical when it comes to contentious matters in the church – like homosexuality. All the churches are having to face up to the reality of gay and lesbian people in the congregations and among the clergy. Because of the fear which exists among so many, the first task of a bishop is to love them into speech, so that they can share their experiences, their stories with him. Loving into speech means that the bishop, for his part, promises there will be no discrimination against them. He will keep silence and listen with all his attention. When he is with his fellow bishops he will then be free to speak and share what he has learnt; and when he meets opposition, as he most certainly will, he will have in his heart the stories of those gay and lesbian priests which will not deter him in his growing conviction that their sexuality, their relationships, their humanity should be publicly recognized, accepted and celebrated.

Those on the 'way up' often sprinkle their conversations with names of well-known people they know they should cultivate to get on. When I was elected to the General Synod I was told that it would be good if I could be seen in the tea room, presumably getting to know influential clergy and laity who might help (or hinder me) on my journey upwards. But a leader whose heart is being educated as I have proposed will give credit to those who have nurtured his spirit; and they will be among those on the edge of society.

I endorse all these precepts; and try with little success to live by them. What makes them so difficult to realize is the obvious fact that leaders are in positions of power: they decide matters which affect the lives of others.

The dilemmas about the 'powerless leader' are beginning to find expression in the Anglican Communion among its five women bishops. Traditionally, bishops – all men – have defined the Church's perception of women, and found the means of controlling them. Bishops have been authoritarian, monarchical and patriarchal in their dealings with men and women. Since February 1989 when Barbara Harris was consecrated as Assistant Bishop in the diocese of Massachusetts, that male barrier has been removed.

The question for women bishops is how they will be able to reconcile the authoritarian office of a bishop with their own memories of struggle against injustice. Will they just abandon these memories and forget their experiences of being ridiculed and ignored, and then as history has shown time and again embark on the oppression of others?

Naturally in time the memories of struggle which ushered in Barbara Harris, Penny Jamieson, Rosemary Kohn, Victoria Matthews and Jane Holmes Dixon will disappear. As more and more women are ordained and then made bishops, their presence will become commonplace. Therefore the experience of these pioneers needs to be treasured.

In a paper 'The bridge too wide', written for the *Virginia Seminary Journal*, the Bishop of Dunedin hints at an answer. She acknowledges the experience of powerlessness and the place of struggle and resistance, but goes on to say: 'Powerlessness knows nothing of the Theology of the Cross: such powerlessness though founded on a respect for the difference of others misses out entirely on the empowerment of the resurrection and is lacking in any generative impulse that would enable it to transform the world.'[3] The Bishop implies that a way of holding together the dilemmas and incompatibilities of the powerless leader is to recognize her task along with others is to work away at the transformation of all things to herald a new creation. It is too early to say how this will work out. We wait and see.[4]

NOTES

1 Morris L. West, *The Shoes of the Fisherman* (New York: Morrow, 1963), p. 66.

2 *The Shoes of the Fisherman*, pp. 66–7.

3 The Rt Revd Penelope Jamieson, Bishop of Dunedin, New Zealand, 'The bridge too wide – women in Christian leadership', *Virginia Seminary Journal* (November 1992).

4 As I write, all the women Anglican Bishops have accepted an invitation to meet together at St James's, Piccadilly, in 1997 to reflect on their leadership.

CHAPTER

6

Ritual

FOR SOME YEARS St James's, Piccadilly has offered hospitality to the New Age Movement: for some time I had had an intuition that one of the reasons why many gather under the generous umbrella of the New Age, or spend large sums of money on all sorts of courses on chanting, meditation and other practices, was a widespread disenchantment with organized religion.

I am not speaking of atheists or of another larger section of society who are indifferent to religion, but of those who have had some connection with the Church – either in childhood or in more limited ways since. They belonged to the Christian community and they left.

Added to that substantial group there is another: those who find themselves drawn to discover what Christianity is about – from a background of indifference and ignorance. This leads to making some sort of commitment, and then after a while they, too, leave. While I was writing this chapter I was told by a solicitor in her mid-thirties, finding herself attached to a struggling congregation in the role of churchwarden and treasurer, 'I did not become a Christian to run a club!'

Over the years I have listened hard to the experiences of these people. I have come to realize, in the midst of all our preoccupations with buildings, management and money, that the churches have neglected their most distinguishing and distinctive activity – worship. Of course, church services are held, Sunday by Sunday and at other times. The Church of England, alongside other denominations, has produced a new Book of Common Prayer called the Alternative Service Book. There are family services, new music, new hymns; in many churches efforts are made to be particularly welcoming. None of these efforts has made much difference to the reaction of the disillusioned – 'boring, irritating and irrelevant'. The disillusionment is an expression of a deep disappointment: 'I had hoped for this, and this is what I experienced.' 'Churchgoers' frequently use the same language. Some may blame themselves for experiencing church services so negatively. It is only loyalty, habit or friends which keep them in church.

Boredom, irritation and irrelevance are the problems. Boredom waits. Boredom is voracious. Once it starts, its appetite is unstoppable. Boredom is contagious. Boredom begins when an audience or congregation begin to wish they were somewhere else. They are not involved in whatever is happening. Seats begin to feel hard, and even in a fairly empty church the congregation feel cramped, hemmed in. Boredom is easily recognized by the level and quality of silence. There is the silence in which five, 500 or 5,000 people hear a pin drop, and there is the silence which never starts, because it is interrupted by coughing and fidgeting.

Sometimes the causes of boredom are obvious: if we cannot see or hear what is happening our attention soon evaporates. But there is another less obvious reason. For 300 years we have understood our relationship to the universe, the earth, and nature in a mechanical way – as a machine to be used, exploited for our own purposes. This way of seeing and describing our experience has been so much part of our mind-set that it may not be surprising that worship has come to be regarded in the same way. The Church speaks of dispensing the sacraments (and I have seen clergy distributing wafers as if they were shelling peas). If sacraments are regarded in this mechanical way then their efficacy does not depend on the character of the priest, but on correct words, said in the correct way, by the correct person. Get the formula right and, hey presto! the bread and wine are changed into the body and blood of Christ.

The metaphor of the universe as a machine can be elaborated as it applies to attitudes to worship. If the universe is regarded as purposeless and soulless, then it follows that we will be satisfied with worship which itself is soulless and bored. If atoms are thought to be inert and lifeless then such inertia will be apparent in worship, and the leaders of worship are not then expected to be passionate, imaginative or life-giving. They are merely required to read the words, and memorize the prayers. If the earth is itself regarded as dead matter, then the earth will not be recognized in worship – except with a nod towards God as our Creator. The Church door is then closed firmly against the earth. With that earthiness, bodies, sweat, sexuality, and exuberance are banished. And when, until recently, it is men who have dominated not only nature and women but also the liturgies, rituals and ceremonies of Christianity, then that completes the experience of much ritual as deadly.

The connection between our perceptions of the universe and the way worship is regarded should not be exaggerated, but it helps to explain the phenomenon of boredom with 'churchgoing', when new perceptions of the earth as a growing, living and changing organism on which we depend for our existence are developing.

Boredom easily turns into irritation. Sometimes the welcome is so urgent, so insistent that we wish we were elsewhere. Sometimes the brain is bombarded with so many words, so many ideas, so much theology, that all we want is quiet. In the Eucharist, before the sermon there may be two hymns, three Bible readings, several prayers – on different and disparate themes.

There are significant reasons for irritation which is to do with the language used. The Book of Common Prayer speaks of God as 'the Sovereign Commander of all the world, in whose hand is power and might, which none is able to withstand' (in Forms of Prayer to be used at Sea), and in Morning Prayer God is addressed as 'O Lord our heavenly Father, high and mighty, King of kings, Lord of lords, the only Ruler of princes' (A Prayer for the Queen's Majesty). In modern liturgies, God is 'Almighty!', God is 'Our Father, which art in Heaven', or 'who art in Heaven', or just 'Our Father in Heaven'. This language of marked masculine transcendence is not the only way God should be described today. Similar questions can be asked about the beautiful prayer for purity which begins the Eucharist in the Book of Common Prayer and the Alternative Service Book.

> Almighty God,
> To whom all hearts are open
> all desires known,
> and from whom no secrets are hidden;
> cleanse the thoughts of our hearts
> by the inspiration of your Holy Spirit,
> that we may perfectly love you,
> and worthily magnify your holy name;
> through Christ our Lord. Amen.

This God is not the utterly transcendent God but the one who is all-knowing, omnipotent, and all-seeing. It is a scary picture.

Anyone finding their way to Christianity for the first time or returning after an absence may not initially be driven by such theological scruples, but sooner or later questions will be raised. If what is said and done does not in some way correspond to what is thought, believed and experienced, then it is hard to argue that such language does not belong to another age.

A clue to what liturgy and, to broaden the subject a little, ritual are about, is to consider the opposite of boredom, irritation and irrelevance. The opposite of boredom is attention. Where there is attentiveness among all those who perform the liturgy and those who participate, everyone's attention is held. There is no fidgeting or shuffling. It is the sort of attention which is experienced on the Centre Court at Wimbledon by the players and the 15,000 or so spectators. It is the experience of those who sing, say, Evensong daily in a cathedral. The congregation are held by the choir, who attend to the music, to one another and to the conductor. At these services the congregation do not always close their eyes, look about, or even follow the words, but look at the choir, themselves absorbed in the music. Because attention of this sort in any context cannot be sustained for long, the event has to allow for moments of relaxation or release.

The opposite of irritation is compliance, or a ready willingness to become accomplices to what is happening. This is the real meaning of participation, not, as is sometimes understood, a variety of different people doing different things. In the same way that a skilled actor can help her audience to believe that a milk bottle is the Leaning Tower of Pisa, so at the liturgy, as the 'churchgoer' comes into the building, takes her prayer book, settles down, she is invited not to enter a make-believe world but to experience herself with others, as a member of a congregation which is part of the Body of Christ.

And the opposite of irrelevance is delight. When rituals work, concentrated energy is released in exactly the same way as in a theatre, where there has been a stunning production. This energy is life-enhancing. It renews and restores. By delight I do not mean the 'feel-good factor'. I mean the experience of joy, and grace, of connections restored, of pain, grief and sin honestly acknowledged, and of vitality and compassion released. Delight, vitality and compassion; these may be experienced, provided there is attention and compliance.

I am beginning to describe the nature of good ritual. Rituals performed with passion and devotion strengthen our capacity to live; they name the despair which is the cause of our apathy, break our addiction to materialism, break through the numbness of our denial to celebrate, savour and rejoice in the basic goodness of life. Celebration waters the soul in its resistance to a world on a course of ecological madness and confusion.

Good rituals emerge from our own backyards, from communities responding to particular challenges in a particular place at a particular time. Kenneth Leech, writing about racism, says:

Connections with other struggles and with wider issues must be made, but they can be made only in the course of activity . . . it is rooted in the worshipping and corporate life of actual communities; it begins with concrete and specific issues and moves outward; and it overcomes the syndrome of a facile optimism in which we seek to deal with problems over too wide an area, at the level of general principles, and moral rhetoric, and then gradually move to a cosmic pessimism, which abandons any hope of change of any kind.[1]

If that is true of racism, then it is true for facing up to all the environmental and ecological challenges as they grow. Rituals disturb our 'desire', which has been co-opted for too long. They nourish an alternative consciousness which informs resistance to those who oppress the marginalized and wound the earth.

Ritual is work. It is not a matter for a liturgical committee to put together a few ideas; it is an integral part of the entire Christian community. By work I mean trying to discover the harmony which is established between the intellect, the emotions and the body. It is rare to find the three components of ourselves working together. If I am speaking about ideas, my intellect is engaged; I will be ignoring my body, and because I want to be as clear as possible, I will keep my feelings under wraps. If I am listening to someone who is in great distress and with whom I empathize, my eyes will be full. I will feel her distress, but I will be ignoring my intellect and my body. If I am driving a car, it is probable that my intellect and emotions will be drifting off, but my body will be, or should be, alert.

Fundamental to establishing this harmony is the body. The body has long been ignored by the churches. All our fears and strictures about nature, sexuality and women have conspired to ignore the body – at least in most European manifestations of Christianity.

How few of us know how to walk, sit, kneel or breathe well. Actors are an exception. They spend many hours training their bodies as do wrestlers, gymnasts and ballet dancers; but the actor's purpose is different to that of the athlete. The actor is concerned to bring together her body and her mind to the part she is playing.

When body, mind and heart come together, there is among all concerned the chance of attentiveness and of transparency through which what is said and done is perceived with clarity. The modern orchestral conductor is the best example of one whose body and emotions and intellect can be perfectly linked. Continually moving the torso, the conductor's body is kept supple – even till very old age.

I know a little about the need to bring the body, mind and emotions together. I was invited to lead the retreat and preach the ordination sermon for the first women to be ordained priests at Hereford Cathedral. My intellect was certainly engaged; I wanted to do the very best for the women and to preach a sermon which was an expression of solidarity for the women and a challenge to everybody else. I spent a week struggling with the biblical texts. My heart was full. For years I had been a member of the Movement for the Ordination of Women, helping here a bit and there a bit. I found the prospect of women priests liberating for me, but my body was not ready – until just before the ceremony. In the Bishop's Palace next to the Cathedral, one of the women to be ordained invited us to stand in a circle; this included the women to be ordained, the Bishop of Hereford and two other bishops, the Dean and Chapter of the Cathedral and other senior clergy. She led us in a simple circle movement, two steps to the side, and one step forward – accompanied to the music of a simple chant, which we sang. Some of the men were slightly clumsy, a little shy. But only for a moment. All of us began to be confident. We moved very slowly, hand in hand, together, round and round. For a time all hierarchy, all patriarchy disappeared – we were together as children of God. As the movement broke up, and we formed into the traditional procession to enter the Cathedral, no group of men or women could have looked or felt more radiant.

There is more skill in the preparation of ritual than the coming together and training of the bodies, hearts and minds of each person. It is the way in which the preachers, the readers, those who tell stories and lead the prayers link what they say to their own inner lives. In *There Are No Secrets*, Peter Brook writes:

> The great storytellers I've seen in teahouses in Afghanistan and Iran recall ancient myths with much joy, but also with inner gravity. At every moment they open themselves to their audiences, not to please them, but to share with them the qualities of a sacred text. In India, the great story-tellers who tell the *Mahabharata* in the temples never lose contact with the grandeur of the myth that they are in the process of reliving. They have an ear turned inwards as well as outwards. This is as it should be for every true actor. It means being in two worlds at the same time.[2]

(For 'actor' read minister or priest.)

The storyteller is open to the audience not in the sense of playing to the gallery, but to share the sacred text which is also part of his own being. The writer of the *Homilies of the Church of England on the Scriptures* puts it like this:

Let us hear, read, and know these holy rules, injunctions, and statutes of our Christian religion, and upon that we have made profession to God at our baptism. Let us with fear and reverence lay up, in the chest of our hearts, these necessary and fruitful lessons. Let us night and day muse, and have meditation and contemplation in them. Let us ruminate, and, as it were, chew the cud, that we may have the sweet juice, spiritual effect, marrow, honey, kernel, taste, comfort and consolation of them. Let us stay quiet, and certify our consciences, with the most infallible certainty, truth, and perpetual assurance of them.[3]

When the words of a ritual or of a sacred text are just read as if they were from a telephone directory, there is no apparent connections between the reader's inner life, and what he is reading. What is missing is that integration of the knowledge of the head and the heart and the words: so the storyteller shares the story with the audience in a way which delights them, but also in a way that delights him. He has made friends with the text. As Peter Brook says, he lives in two worlds at once.

What will rituals look like and be about? Traditionally, rituals manage change: that is one of the functions of the rites of passage – birth, marriage and death. Most change involves a range of experiences, from loss and confusion, to grief and chaos, and one of the purposes of ritual is to see that this 'in-between time' – that is between leaving the past behind, either voluntarily or involuntarily, and before a new thing emerges – is cherished and guarded.[4] It resembles the process of mourning: if that is too hastily dealt with or even denied there is no recovery, healing or vitality.

It is strange that there are so few rituals for change – for the break-up of a relationship or signalling a divorce, for redundancy, retirement, moving house, changing jobs, marking family occasions. It is strange, too, that institutions have no rituals to mark their own change; as I have said, the Church of England will have to face up to a time of great pain and confusion; one of the signs of a mature and wise leadership is that it will guard the chaos and not be too much in a hurry to get to the next stage. Anger, dismay, loss of our own identity and purpose are bound to surface as churches discover they have to increasingly fend for themselves: life is not what it was. I have met Roman Catholics who still resent the way the Mass in English was foisted upon them. They grieve for the old days, but there is no way in which grief can be expressed; so it is left snarling and un-acknowledged. I have met Anglicans who have been treated in a similar way about the disappearance of the Book of Common Prayer.

And above all, rituals will emerge to handle our despair about a hope for the earth. Ours is the first generation which has a sense that the planet will end: we will not pull through, and the future is cancelled. To own up to this colossal sense of loss invites more than therapy or the occasional Despair workshop (there are such things!); it requires a liturgical and ritual setting, where the dislocation, even some sort of madness, is acknowledged.

Such personal or institutional rituals, or those which touch the future of our planet, acknowledge that it is human, or natural, to sense the dis-integration of the future; they will be characterized by times of waiting, letting go of our daily certainties; and in that darkness, and not soon, allow-ing images of hope to form. Rituals are not solitary, but opportunities for discovering our strength together, so that there are within the community resources for the struggle among us all.

The fundamental stance of all ritual is thanksgiving – not, in the first place, for the person of Christ, but simply for the universe that is. We are neither self-made, nor self-sufficient. All life is a gift. Each human life, and the life of everything else. Thanksgiving is evoked by awe of the diversity, grandeur and intricacy of creation; such attention and mindfulness must provide the framework for all liturgy and ritual. From the official service books, this element is missing. For example, in the most solemn moment of the Prayer of Thanksgiving in which the bread and wine are blessed, the celebrant begins the prayer with the words:

> It is indeed right,
> it is our duty and our joy,
> at all times and in all places
> to give you thanks and praise,
> holy Father, heavenly King,
> almighty and eternal God,

and then moves immediately to Christ:

> through Jesus Christ your only Son our Lord.

There is no awareness of thanksgiving for the ongoing and extraordinary process of creation before the emergence of the human species.

The understanding of creation as the theatre of God's glory is not new. In *Original Blessing*, Matthew Fox unearths a buried and submerged tradition which provides a necessary corrective, at least for Protestantism; Protestantism has elevated the crucifixion as the primary self-disclosure of God at the expense of history and nature; in its most extreme form these are no more than a backdrop. But useful as this tradition is, it is not enough.

The energies of artists of every sort, and those who are not professional, need to be invited to express thanksgiving today.

There is, however, a difficulty with thanksgiving and the praise of God. Part of my duties is to officiate at memorial services. There is no set form, and they involve a considerable amount of preparation. A recurring difficulty is what to sing together. Sometimes I propose 'Praise my soul, the King of Heaven'. This is a fine adaptation of Psalm 103 by Henry Lyte. It is a suitable hymn for a congregation which might include agnostics, and people of other faiths, because the hymn includes no reference to Jesus Christ.

The penultimate line of each verse has the words 'Praise Him, praise Him' (sometimes changed in modern versions to 'Alleluia, Alleluia'); the last lines echo the theme of praise: 'Praise the everlasting King', 'Glorious in His faithfulness', 'Widely as His mercy flows', 'Praise the high Eternal one', and 'Praise with us the God of grace'. Occasionally comments are made about the exclusively masculine imagery in the hymns, but more frequently the question is 'Why do you need to keep on praising God?' or 'What's wrong with this God who needs so much praising?' (I am reminded of a cartoon where a voice from Heaven addresses the congregation: 'It's nice of you to say that – say it again!') There seems to be something unhealthy about such a God, whether a tyrant who needs to be appeased or a more benign presence who enjoys being flattered.

What has been missing from these popular perceptions of praise is any awareness of creation which may evoke, in a religious person, a mindfulness and awe – properly expressed in praise.

But thanksgiving is not just thanksgiving for creation as the theatre for the story of God. Retold just like that is to ignore another narrative, and that is the story of Jesus Christ. The relationship between the incarnation and creation is complex, and beyond the scope of this book, and certainly beyond a chapter on ritual. But this can be said: Jesus Christ in the official liturgies of the Eucharist is too abstract, too one-dimensional, too generalized a figure. He is like a formula, and as such he has little place in the scheme of things which I have sketched. We need rituals which affirm our intuition that Jesus Christ sums up, makes clear what is already present, however obscurely, in the universe: Jesus Christ – his life, death, resurrection and ascension – focuses intensely what is already present and operating dimly in the universe. This is the thinking behind the nature of what is called the Cosmic Christ – so that it is possible to say that from the beginning of the universe, Christ is already present as an outgoing redeeming and transfiguring Word.

Thanksgiving is shrouded in pain; it acknowledges that pain, even death, is a gift of God. It is this startling understanding of the way things are that is behind the tradition of Irish Celtic and Catholic religion. 'Tis a fine day – thanks be to God.' 'Tis a wild day – thanks be to God.' Or when Mary Casey in Synge's *Riders to the Sea* learns of the death of her sons by drowning, she utters the prayer 'Blessed be the Holy Will of God'. The terrible sea had taken her two sons, helpless as two new-born babies in their strong boast of manhood. These beliefs arose out of poverty and famine. Their stoicism is not to be confused with fatalism, because there is a dignity, nobility and even humour here which can release generosity of spirit.

Part of what I am describing is a felt need to push out the boundaries of our official liturgies to reflect and include everything. I have been inspired by the writings of Teilhard de Chardin, particularly his *Mass of the Earth*. One day in China, he was alone in the desert on the Feast of the Transfiguration. He wished to celebrate the Eucharist but he had no bread, no wine.

> When Christ says: 'This is my body', these words extend beyond the morsel of bread over which they are said. They give birth to the whole mystical body of Christ. The effect extends beyond the consecrated host to the cosmos itself – the entire realm of matter is slowly but irresistibly affected by this great consecration.

This understanding of the Mass seems to me to be exaggerated, and to claim too much. But the way the Eucharist is invariably celebrated gives no hint of such claims. But there is truth in it, and I have tried to reflect this in the way the Eucharist is celebrated on occasions at St James's, Piccadilly.

The Eucharist consists of four actions. The offering, consecrating, breaking and sharing of the bread and wine. The Offertory includes the offering of bread, wine and money – all the material things of our existence. They are then blessed and broken. Before the sharing, there is the breaking – as if in a mysterious way a sacrificial life generates seeds of generosity and goodness in the secret processes of transformation. But the Eucharist is not just a symbolic meal for a local ecclesiastical community; it makes a public statement about the renewal and healing of the planet. And the breaking is the place where this is made explicit. The community have gathered round the Table, and after the consecrating of the bread and wine, the celebrant turns to the East, raises the bread and says:

To the East:

This bread is broken in honour of all those who love God – our sisters and brothers who worship the God of the Hindus and follow the path of the Buddha, for our sisters and brothers in Islam and the Jewish people from whom we come.

> To all these be honour and blessing
> in the breaking of this bread;
> and we pray that one day we may be one.

To the South:

This bread is broken in honour of the green blue Earth and all the elements of water, fire and air that surround and support her:

> Mother Earth, despoiled, plundered and ravaged by our greed
> yet alive and green,
> To the Earth be honour and blessing in the breaking of the
> Bread; and we pray that one day the scars will be no more.

To the West:

This bread is broken in honour of the broken and dispossessed

> and for all those who have no bread
> that one day this earth will be a home for all humanity – a
> room at the Inn for all.

To the North:

This bread is broken in honour of the brokenness of each one of us:

> the child within us broken by cruelty or coldness
> the adult broken by loneliness or failure
> our health broken by sickness or loss

> To each one here be honour and blessing
> warmth and abundance
> in the breaking of the Bread of Life.
> We pray that one day we will know the wholeness
> that is of Christ.

And then, turning back to the Table, the celebrant raises the bread, breaks it for the last time and says:

> We break this bread
> to share in the body of Christ

and the people say:

'Though we are many, we are one body
because we all share in one bread.'

The traditional celebration of baptism of children or adults gives no
sense of welcoming those to be baptized into the universe or into a living
relationship with the earth and its creatures. Therefore I take the child in
my arms, or lead the adult out into the church garden to meet the rest of
the world, to introduce her as if for the first time to the plants, flowers,
the trees, the insects, the birds and to the clouds and the sun, on which
our whole existence depends. It is a simple ritual act, and of itself does
little except as a signal to break down the alienation between ourselves and
the natural environment.

There is much else which emerges as creation-centred rituals come into
being – freedom in the way in which God is addressed, the disappearance
of hierarchy and patriarchy in the interest of inclusiveness, reminders of
creation's gorgeous diversity and of our connectedness and interdependence. The place of blessing will be restored, and the whole will reflect an
affirmation of, and delight in, the earth.

However, such rituals are only part of the story. If liturgy has ignored
or rejected nature, it has also reduced humanity. As I have often been told,
'When I come to church I feel as if I have to leave my emotions outside,
except those which surround my guilt – no one seems to bother about
what I am thinking or feeling; sooner or later, it gets to be meaningless
and I just wonder why I put up with it or why I bother to go!'

One of the reasons for this is that Christianity has ignored the Jewish
tradition of lamentation; the basic text for the expression of Lamentation
is in the story of the Exodus:

After a long time the King of Egypt died. The Israelites groaned under
their slavery, and cried out. Out of the slavery their cry for help rose
up to God. God heard their groaning, and God remembered his
covenant with Abraham, Isaac and Jacob. God looked upon the
Israelites, and God took notice of them. (Exod 2.23–25 NRSV)

A careful first-time reader will be wondering what will happen after the
Pharaoh's death; after such suffering, over such a long time, is there a
chance for a new regime? No, is the answer: if anything, the plight of the
Hebrew slaves increases. They cry out to God, and God hears their cries,
remembering his promises, looks upon them, takes notice of them (and
eventually frees them!).

In the Exodus story, the slaves summon God away from his distant throne to join human life. They call on God to be fully present, and, as it were, to move in with them. They believe that God can be mobilized by their cries. The crying and the groaning is empowering. The slaves begin to realize that the Pharaoh's power is fraudulent, that the present order has to be broken up, that life and liberation is bestowed without benefit of kings. The Hebrew slaves organize themselves and in their groaning to God begin to name their pain, and recognize the truth and possibilities for their liberation.

Today lamentation has to find a place in our ritual: coming together in the struggle for a more just, more humane, a more ecologically-based world – as that struggle finds expression locally, regionally, nationally and internationally. Communities will begin to 'cry to God'.

Lamentation is a strange activity. I have been involved in several attempts to create rituals of lamentation on environmental matters. They have had the reverse effect to what was intended because they were little more than a recital of all environmental disasters. Guilt and powerlessness compete, and nothing happens. Lamentation operates at a different level, where the language is more vivid, specific and local. It assumes a community which has arisen or grown out of its sense of outrage and its desire to combat some named injustice – whether it is racism or the perpetrators of environmental degradation. Such a community searches for allies and calls on God.

Calling on God (in the Exodus narrative, the Psalms, some of the Prophets, and in the shattering cry of dereliction in the Gospels: 'My God, My God, why hast thou forsaken me?') seems a quaint, outmoded, even primitive way of relating to God. Its perception of God as a deaf, lazy, sleepy and certainly unreliable Father hardly matches with the God of formalized Christian dogma – say as in the doctrine of the Trinity. But, as we saw in the chapter on *chutzpah*, talking to God is set in the context of the covenant, which perceives reality in its ambiguity and uncertainty, out of which we are addressed by a mysterious other. This 'other' is an endlessly inscrutable mystery and endlessly problematic for us. The prepositions and language about God in this matter, which reflect God's distance from us, (over, beyond and above us) can be interchanged with those of God who is called from out of the deep, or in the powerful images of interconnectedness.

Therefore in rituals there is no need to be shy of such language. When lamentation is created, then numerous opportunities and necessities for ritual emerge. Instead of penitence being the bland, desultory prayer as we have it in the modern prayer book, it becomes the occasion for acknowledging collusion with the powers, our faintheartedness and lack of courage, as well as for those whom we have hurt in the community, although we should not underestimate the difficulties of creating penitential language which does justice to the enormity of, say, the Holocaust.

We will begin to recognize what our interrelatedness means, that we start to treat one another as part of who we are, rather than as those with whom we are in constant competition – not so much enemies as unconverted friends.

Despair can give way to cynicism, and it is easy enough to settle for violence or comfort. But the Exodus story points to something else – a new sense of freedom, as the power of enslavement has been terminated: 'Sing to the Lord, for he has triumphed gloriously; horse and rider he has thrown into the sea.' The Bible, the Christian tradition and experience point to the promise and hope of restoration. Exile is the place where there is homecoming.

I have described the ways in which two aspects of the Christian tradition, that of the Cosmic Christ and of the Covenant and Kingdom of God, are the structures around which new liturgies can be created. The Cosmic Christ tradition is horizontal, intimate, mysterious, encompassing and encircling. The Covenant tradition intrudes with its insistent concern for justice and the mute victim of our greed – the earth. And at the point where the horizontal and vertical meet, there is released much imagination, power and energy needed for the work of healing the planet.

Few of us will recognize the liturgies and rituals I have been describing. They are not part of what 'churchgoing' means; and in spite of the fundamentally traditional basis out of which good ritual should emerge, any Christian community which begins to work on ritual in the ways I am proposing will soon find themselves in trouble with bishops and among the more entrenched members of their own communities. What is to be done?

I have been inspired by the Catholic Women's Network. These are Roman Catholic women who believe priests should be married, if they wish, and that women should be ordained. They are loyal Catholics; none of them I know would consider becoming Anglican. Many are Catholics since birth, cradle Catholics, but they also arrange their own rituals and celebrations, including lay celebration of the Mass. If there is a problem about this it lies with the authorities and not with the women. No doubt as their voices are raised more publicly and more join them, calls will be made for them to be ostracized and even excommunicated. These women have to live split lives. It is not easy living between two worlds. They are a model for those, like myself, who wish to remain loyal to their own roots in the Church, but at the same time want and will create powerful, new rituals and communities. These are the threshold communities, acknowledging their roots and their past, but looking forward to the future.

The Catholic Women's Network is a community; its members know one another; they bother about each other. They are not quitters; and they will not go away. They are an alternative community on the edge of the Roman Catholic Church.

I have a closer link with another community 'on the edge'. This is with the leaders of a group of about 200 people in their twenties and thirties. Their roots are Evangelical, but over the years they have moved on, not discovering their roots so much as expanding their horizons, particularly in their concern for justice and the Kingdom of God, and also recognizing creation as a gift, and not simply a backdrop to work out their own faith. Their passion is to worship in the ambience of their own culture – that of the rave night club, relying on video technology. They do not feel at home using the authorized service of the churches. On the other hand, they wish to stay within the Church of England. They are another 'threshold' community looking backwards to where they come from, but also moving into the future.

Threshold communities – tiny and fragile as they are – are often seen as a threat or a problem by church authorities. There is a wish not often expressed that they would go away. But I see them as communities where powerful rituals are fashioned from which the rest of us have a lot to learn.

NOTES

1 Kenneth Leech, *Subversive Orthodoxy – Traditional Faith and Radical Commitment* (Toronto: Anglican Book Centre, 1992), p. 28. See also his *We Preach Christ Crucified* (London: Darton, Longman and Todd, 1994) and *Struggle in Babylon – Racism in the Cities and Churches of Britain* (London: Sheldon Press, 1988).
2 Peter Brook, *There Are No Secrets – Thoughts on Acting and Theatre* (London: Methuen, 1993), p. 31.
3 *The Homilies of the Church of England on the Scriptures* (first book published 1547; second book published 1563: reprinted by the Church Society).
4 'Guarded' from Hannah Ward and Jennifer Wild, *Guard the Chaos – Finding Meaning in Change* (London: Darton, Longman and Todd, 1995). The authors (both Anglicans) are involved in Womenspace, a programme of events 'for women to gather around issues of religion and spirituality', held at Websters, a Christian women's centre in London.

CHAPTER

7

The Bible and a sermon

FOR MANY YEARS I have asked all sorts of people from every walk of life a simple question, 'Do you read the Bible?' I have asked Christians and Jews, agnostics and atheists – young, middle-aged and the elderly. I have asked those who ridicule Christianity as well as those who have no time for organized religion, but would hesitate to call themselves atheists.

The unanimity of the responses has been striking. First, there is resentment at being asked such a direct question; after all, it is none of my business. Then questions to me as to why I was asking about the Bible, and then the answers came: 'No, I don't read the Bible . . . used to when I was young . . . well, I'm not much of a scholar . . . don't read anything much as it happens, bit on holiday and last thing at night, that sort of thing.'

Sometimes as part of a more extended conversation I caught a hankering about the Bible, almost a sense of loss as we talked. They would like to be able to read it, but how to go about it?

This question has become a problem for many whom I have welcomed at St James's, Piccadilly. With barely any knowledge of religion they come to learn about Christianity; trying to understand the doctrines of the Church. It is not an easy task. Coming up against the Bible adds to their difficulties. Some announce that they are going to read the Bible from cover to cover, sensing that it was going to be a bit of an obstacle race, and then a few weeks later, and a hundred pages on, they give up, invariably at Leviticus.

The disappearance of the Bible from European culture is self-evident; once it was part of the intellectual and imaginative make-up of poets and posers, novelists and artists. Even if only a few knew the original languages in which the Bible was written, there was at least for the English-speaking community the King James Bible – 'that old tongue' with its 'clang and fervour' as the critic Edmund Wilson described it. Now even that, as I discovered, has disappeared: our culture today does not value reading, let alone reading books written before 1900, and ancient, religious books – like the Bible.

The loss of the Bible in European Christianity is, however, another matter. It seems an absurd, perverse statement to make: after all, Sunday by Sunday the Bible is read aloud; preachers are required to expound the text. Every brand of Christian – conservative, liberal and radical – appeals to the Bible to legitimize their attitudes and opinions. Every sort of theology, ecclesiastical reports by synods, and devotional books – all use the Bible. But in spite of this deference to the Bible, all my experience adds up to this: outside the circle of experts, there is considerable confusion and widespread ignorance. Whatever the churches say about the Bible, and the claims they make about it in its liturgies and pronouncements, their words have fallen on deaf ears.

As Robert Lowell in his poem 'Waking early Sunday morning' puts it:

> O Bible, chopped and crucified
> In hymns we hear, but do not read.[1]

Any considerations of the Bible and the imagination begin from its disappearance from our culture and Christianity.

The reason for its disappearance can be found in my own experience of the Bible. I have not had those shattering experiences of St Augustine or John Bunyan, whose lives were changed totally by the Bible, but there are elements in my own reaction to the Bible which many others have shared.

I possess a family Bible which my father inherited. It is called the Illustrated Household Commentary, and the preface says that it is 'particularly valuable to heads of families in conducting domestic worship'. My father had faint memories of household prayers in the family home at Croessnydd Hall, near Wrexham, where my grandfather was a Victorian squire: the household would gather in the dining room, and morning prayers would be said. But my parents and family had no interest in the Church or Christianity.

At Sherborne I experienced compulsory chapel, but as a young organist I was more interested in music than in anything else. Only one passage from the Bible remains in my mind from my schooldays – 'Let us now praise famous men' (Ecclesiasticus 44.1–15), read every year at the Commemoration Service.

I have already described my bizarre encounter with the Bible as a Cambridge undergraduate. But I had one other experience of books and reading at Cambridge which has remained with me. Professor David Daiches lectured on James Joyce's *Ulysses*. Whereas many of his colleagues in the English faculty lectured from well-used notes, David Daiches arrived with *Ulysses*, and led us into the book, chapter by chapter. He was enthusiastic, knowledgeable and utterly dedicated to James Joyce. He made us want to go back to the text and, among all its many difficulties, discover it for ourselves. Where are the preachers and teachers who have that similar informed dedication, passion and love for the Bible?

My first serious encounter with the Bible was my conversion to Christianity. The Bible had nothing to do with this event, clearly, since my relationship to it had been more or less non-existent, and my indifference and ignorance of it was similar to the experience of many today.

Then, at Cuddesdon Theological College, I started a serious study of the Bible. There was little time to read it; a useful short cut was to read what others had said about it. At this point I was introduced to biblical criticism. By criticism, I do not mean niggling, but a process of understanding about the nature of these ancient texts. This was most exhilarating; insofar as I had thought about how the books of the Bible had come to be written, I imagined that they had been written by divine dictation. Now, it was intoxicating to savour the efforts of those who treated the Bible as any other ancient text. Thus I learnt about the varieties of biblical criticism – the oral tradition, form criticism, source and textual criticism, historical criticism: all these disciplines aimed to help the reader to understand the Bible in its own setting, how the books came to be, how reliable they were as history, and how the sources of different books were put together. For me, and for many of my contemporaries, this was all news, and good news, for it meant that it was reasonable, intellectually possible and sensible to be Christian.

Biblical scholarship invigorated my thinking for some years. But when I became the vicar of a large housing estate in South London I began to feel uneasy. Something was missing.

At Cuddesdon, in seminars on preaching, we were told to forget all what we had learnt about biblical criticism and just preach the gospel. Since the sermon was supposed to interpret the Scriptures, we were left facing a problem which was not recognized and therefore not addressed. It was this failure to make connections between the worlds of scholarship and life which has brought the Bible into disrepute. Biblical criticism was fine in the study, but what happens to the Bible outside the study? Not much, was the answer.

Biblical scholarship requires the detachment, neutrality and objectivity of the best detective. I am a reader of thrillers and detective stories – of Patricia Highsmith, Ruth Rendell and P. D. James – and my work on the Bible required a similar approach, sniffing around for the truth, testing hypotheses, following every trail until I could sort out the true from the false. The scholar, like the detective, sifts out the evidence, tests theories, looks for proof – all to discover 'what really happened'. The text is worked over, analysed bit by bit in the hope that the truth will be revealed. Of course, once the murderer is arrested, the detective's job is done, and the story ends. But with the Bible, the task is more elusive, and the results less certain.

The difficulties about the Bible have come about because the reader has lost confidence in the text. She has come to view the text with suspicion because she has a sure sense that it can no longer be trusted. She will not be well versed in biblical scholarship, but rumours of the quarrying and subsequent erosion will have reached her. And without that trust that the words before her eyes are communicating what they say they are, communication breaks down. And this is what has happened to the Bible, and has turned it into such a problematic and puzzling book.

Here are some elementary examples of what I mean. Although the Bible says that Genesis is the 'first book of Moses', we know Moses did not write it, any more than David wrote most of the Psalms, or St Paul all the Letters ascribed to him. Although the Bible says that Matthew, Mark and Luke were the authors of their Gospels, we know this is not so – they were, in fact, written anonymously. Although Genesis describes the creation of the world in six days, we know now not only that this is not so, but that the writers did not mean what they said.

We know that the Nativity stories are not historical accounts of the birth of Jesus, but meditations on the significance of the birth of the Messiah. We have learnt that the predictions of the death of Christ in the Gospels were added after the resurrection. We know, now, that Jesus may have been mistaken about the second coming.

These examples (and they are not exceptional, and are generally agreed) do not add up to much on their own, but cumulatively they, and many contentious findings of biblical scholarship, have the effect of dismantling the text. One of the latest, most readable and more complicated examples of what I am trying to say is found in E. P. Sanders and Margaret Davies, *Studying the Synoptic Gospels.* This book considers in some detail all the available evidence about the Gospels of Matthew, Mark and Luke. It examines what is known of the views of the authors or editors of the three Gospels; it considers all the evidence about the sources of the Gospels, and the extent to which they relate to each other. It considers 'form' criticism

– the analysis of each fragment, each story on its own terms – its development from one Gospel to another, and its place in each Gospel. It considers a variety of literary approaches (which underplay the historical context and content). They place the Gospels in their setting, comparing their particular genre to contemporary literature, and analyse the use of the Old Testament and the New.

At the centre of this maze, on the last page, the authors say:

This is what we can know about his mission, and about his view of the 'Kingdom':

1. Jesus expected 'the kingdom of God' either as a dramatic cosmic event, or as a new social order – or both, one leading to the other.
2. He saw his own mission as being the call of Israel to the kingdom.
3. He meant the inclusion of all Israel, both the lost ten tribes (note the symbolism of the twelve disciples) *and* the present 'lost sheep of the house of Israel'.
4. He saw his work as continuing John's, but with a difference. John preached repentance and practised abstinence. Jesus sought sinners, did not dwell on their failings, and was known as one who ate and drank with them.
5. He believed that love of the neighbour included not only love of the outcast, but also love of the enemy.
6. He did not himself call Gentiles, but this was a reasonable continuation of his work.
7. He thought that the new order demanded new ethical standards, and he (for example) forbade or strongly discouraged divorce, possibly looking to the order of creation as the standard of the new age.[2]

They add that more, probably, can be known about Jesus, but these seven points are as true as anything can be.

Thus the attentive reader has not only to read the words before her, but to become aware of a sub-text – which is really what is going on, and about which scholarship can enlighten her – through analysis and dissection of the text, chapter by chapter, verse by verse, phrase by phrase: the biblical commentary is the embodiment of this process. Nowhere is the imagination involved in this reading and study. The appeal is to the intellectual side of our nature, not to our imagination.

There are few readers who want to be theological sleuths – but how else could we read the Bible? There seemed to be no other options available; as an inexperienced preacher I remember 'unpacking' the readings for the day, and leaving them in bits, with a lame attempt at the end of the sermon to make some sort of link with the contemporary world. Thus it is that the Bible has been virtually abandoned and taken over by the universities, theological faculties and departments of biblical studies. The clergy at a crucial period in their training are left bereft of any systematic method in reading and interpreting.

I have not detected any conspiracy among biblical scholars to take the Bible away from the rest of us. Their situation is understandable: university departments have a vested interest in ensuring that research and scholarship are continued. And with the 'market' determining most of the way our institutions run, the pressure to produce more research does not let up. Inevitably any form of specialization develops its own jargon and language.

Inevitably there are sharp differences and shifting authorities. Moreover, academics argue, and rightly, that it is not their responsibility to see how the Bible fares outside their work; that, they say, is not their business. But outside that circle, everyone else is easily dismayed, mystified and ultimately defeated. That is why the Bible has all but disappeared, and why the imagination has had no place in the consideration and study of the Bible.

The comedienne Anna Russell, in her classic exposition of Wagner's *Ring*, put it simply. She says that the endless analysis of Wagner's operas are written 'by some great experts for the edification of other great experts, but these are usually so esoteric as to leave the average person as befogged as before, and in fact tend to discourage him from going to the opera altogether'.

Then I heard Alec McCowen reading St Mark's Gospel; my eyes were opened again.

It was a relief to hear a whole book recited, in contrast to the detailed studying of verses and phrases which I had been led to believe was the way to the correct reading of the Bible. This was followed by Paul Alexander's St John's Gospel, and Roger Rees's Revelation. I began to get a sense of what these books were like in their entirety. In 1983, now in Piccadilly, I arranged a public reading of the Bible from Genesis to Revelation – without a break. (It takes 99 hours.) The reading was a fund-raising event for Church Action on Poverty; the readers were mostly well-known public figures, politicians and actors. It was touching to note how the readers had taken time and trouble to prepare their readings, even those who were landed with some of the genealogies and other unpromising material. Those who sat through as much of this as they could – many slept in the church – found many of the readings absorbing, sometimes abrasive, and occasionally healing.

Then during the 1970s I learnt that there were places other than the study where the Bible was read. Through the writings of Leonardo Boff, Gustavo Gutiérrez and Jon Sobrino, I learnt how, in Central and South America, the Bible enriched and generated hope among those who lived under oppressive regimes.

Through writing and meeting feminist theologians I learnt how women brought their own experience of the misogyny and patriarchy of the Church to the Bible. Some left the Church exasperated with what they discovered there; others have found in the Bible a thread of hopeful memories where women in a man's world were vindicated.

What I have learnt from liberation and feminist theologians is that they bring the totality of their experience and that of their communities to the reading of the Bible. Whereas I had been taught to analyse the Bible objectively, ignoring the imagination. I began to see that the Bible yielded more when it was addressed, interrogated and challenged. I began to see how necessary it was for a reader to be conscious of the place from which she was looking, thinking, speaking and doing. Thus how the Bible looks depends on where you stand.

Imagine you are a donkey – and a donkey who can read – what do you make of the Bible? Probably not much; although you know how indispensable you are to the existence of your society, this is not recognized by the Bible; and when you are mentioned, you do not have a name, except insofar as you are identified with your owner. However, if I was a donkey I would be encouraged by at least two stories – the first is the story of Balaam's donkey in Numbers 22. The donkey recognized, in a way that Balaam did not, what God was up to. Balaam was furious with the donkey, who when confronted with the angel of God standing on the road with a drawn sword, first turned off the road and made off across country, and then, after another appearance of the angel in a narrow lane, injured Balaam's foot against a wall, and, at a final appearance of the angel in the narrowest of lanes, just lay down with Balaam on top of her. Balaam is furious: the donkey has made such a fool of him. He beats her: the donkey protests. She has always been reliable ever since Balaam's youth – why beat her? Balaam does not quite apologize, but agrees that the donkey had never let him down. Balaam emerges from this story as arrogant and foolish; the donkey as prudent and loyal. That would have cheered the heart of any donkey, not least because Balaam was a powerful prince.

And, secondly, in the Gospels, the donkey would no doubt have felt highly privileged because it was she, an ordinary, domestic animal (not the horse associated with military prowess), who carried Jesus into Jerusalem on Palm Sunday. So, according to the donkey logic there are hints of an alternative tradition in the Bible about donkeys which does honour them after all!

*   *   *

At the very least then, I had to learn to bring my concerns, preoccupations and questions to the text, as clearly and consciously as possible. It is not possible to abandon our values as we read. It may be argued that this throws out all the neutrality and objectivity of the scholar, but scholarship is not neutral: it has its own value system, exalting the rational over the emotional, the intellect over the imagination – its own 'political' values of an essentially conservative nature, socializing students into its own methods and pre-occupations, and until recently being the sole preserve of white, middle-class males.

Then, reading has to happen in such a way that the text is allowed to breathe and to speak – in the way that Alec McCowen's St Mark's Gospel did. Reading the Bible is tough and delicate – bringing together the reader's passion, and the strangeness of the text; and there has always to be enough room for the text to address the reader, even as the reader wrestles with the text.

Reading the Bible needs to be preceded by a sense of anticipation, that it will yield some hope and truth. And in the reading, the reader has to both bring her questions, and also suspend her everyday beliefs, so that she can enter into this strangest of worlds – similar preparations to those which we bring as members of an audience at the opera or the theatre.

What I am proposing is a way of reading which is essentially naive, so that the reader is prepared to become vulnerable and open to change.

A word needs to be added about how the text relates to the reader, since I have emphasized how the reader relates to the text. A first-time reader, whose curiosity about the Bible is growing, will regard large parts of the Bible as any other literature: in the narratives, the questions about plot and character arise; in the historical books, the reader needs to have some sense of the purpose and function of the 'history'. In the more strictly theological books (like St Paul's Letters), the ideas which are expressed need to be seen in their own context. Taking stories, history or theology out of their context invariably destroys the original sense. Sometimes a context is unknown or ignored, and the meaning of what is written is quite distorted. For example, one of the phrases of Apollo carved in stone at Delphi was 'Know thyself'. Today this is taken as a call to introspection – know what is within yourself; but in the ancient Greek world, long before Freud, it meant simply 'Know your limits and do not be guilty of presumption'. Introspection does not come into it.

The reader will therefore want to develop a sharp, historical imagination so that she begins to have a sense of the context of the ancient world, along-side her own preoccupations and concerns.

Perhaps reclaiming this ancient literature in the way I am proposing is just too big a task. Is it worth it? May not our culture and Christianity be right in letting the Bible slip away? Rumours about the strange book will keep its memory alive in the study and among some marginal groups within the churches. Meanwhile, the churches get along well enough without it, and, after all, have we not always made Christ in our own image?

At formative periods of Christianity, the Bible was not involved. The creeds were composed without the benefit of the complete Canon; the Romano-British Church was the first considerable church in Britain, established well before St Augustine. All the Christians had then were the Gospels and a few psalms.

Furthermore, biblical scholarship has rightly alerted us to the strangeness of this Oriental world – of slavery, xenophobia, misogyny, and rules and regulations about a tiny community. Here, in this world, there are kings and concubines, giants, witches, and angels everywhere – far removed from our own day. And in the New Testament what emerges at the end of it are tiny communities, scattered about in a few Mediterranean cities, banned by the Roman emperor as a threat to law and order.

But I have persisted. To give in would be to contribute to the barbarism and brutalizing of our imagination, and as a Christian I want to find within the Bible a sense of a living word that is from God and of God. I have discovered what a dangerous book the Bible is. How it threatens organized religion, how it holds up a mirror to our endless capacity to be greedy, how consistently it reminds us of the dignity of the human being, especially the poorest, and how it offers extraordinary pictures of the possibilities and hopes of a new world – the Kingdom of God.

And in among all this, I have found a density and opacity – a deep mystery in which the writers share their sense of a transcending God disclosed among the vagaries and unpredictable arena of our history. I have come to love the Bible.

*   *   *

A SERMON

I have already mentioned how I have used the Bible in preaching, and how mediocre the results were. Twenty years on, I have discovered the Bible in the way I have described; as a result I have radically altered my attitude to preaching in as far as it concerns the use of biblical texts.

The best way to illustrate what I am saying is to consider how a particular sermon came into being, and how the Bible played its part.

The occasion for this sermon was an event I have already referred to – the ordination of the first fifteen women deacons to be made priest in Hereford Cathedral. There were three set texts: the first from Isaiah, chapter 61:

> The spirit of the Lord God is upon me,
> because the Lord has anointed me;
> he has sent me to bring good
> news to the oppressed,
> to bind up the brokenhearted,
> to proclaim liberty to the captives,
> and release to the prisoners;
> to proclaim the year of the Lord's favour,
> and the day of vengeance of our God;
> to comfort all who mourn;
> to provide for those who mourn in Zion –
> to give them a garland instead of ashes,
> the oil of gladness instead of mourning,
> the mantle of praise instead of a faint spirit. (RSV)

The second was from Romans, chapter 12, of which the key verses are:

I appeal to you therefore, brothers and sisters, by the mercies of God, to present your bodies as a living sacrifice, holy and acceptable to God, which is your spiritual worship. Do not be conformed to this world, but be transformed by the renewing of your minds, so that you may discern what is the will of God – what is good and acceptable and perfect. (RSV)

And the Gospel reading was from St John, chapter 20, part of the Easter story, ending with the words of the risen Christ to his disciples in the locked room:

Jesus said to them again, 'Peace be with you. As the Father has sent me, so I send you.' When he had said this, he breathed on them and said to them, 'Receive the Holy Spirit. If you forgive the sins of any, they are forgiven them; if you retain the sins of any, they are retained.' (RSV)

Confronted with these three dense and difficult texts, my initial reaction was to ignore them because they seemed to have nothing in common with each other, and nothing to say which was appropriate for the ordination of women.

I persevered, and began by looking closely at the second reading, which I happened to know best. St Paul is saying that the gospel requires a transformation of the way we live, and the rest of the reading explains what a transformed life and community looks like. Because the ordination of women had broken a barrier, I was interested to see what the transformed life had to say about barriers. And sure enough, verse 19 – 'Beloved, never avenge yourself' – implies that to conform to the world means to practise vengeance, and that is to deliberately exclude those who, for whatever reason, do not fit. But the transformed world of which Paul speaks happens when the stranger is welcomed and received, as in verse 13 he urges his readers 'to extend hospitality to strangers'!

The mandate for welcoming and hospitality, I remembered, has an ancient history, all the way back to the deliverance of the slaves out of Egypt, to the creators of a new and revolutionary community under a covenant with God. The memory that these people were once excluded and outsiders under Pharaoh was only just kept alive by the prophets who reminded kings of their responsibility to welcome the outsider.

I remembered again that this mandate was renewed in the ministry of Jesus. The first reading, from Isaiah, was the text of his keynote sermon recorded in Luke's Gospel.[3] But Jesus' sermon and the text of Isaiah were formed out of an astonishing act of public imagination in which every 50 years all land was to be returned to its owners, and all debts cancelled. This was the year of Jubilee which says the fabric of society has to be preserved to protect the weak from the strong. It is the inclusion of all, and the reversal of everything that is inhumane and unjust, that makes the Jubilee radical.

I began to see a clear link between the first two readings: the requirement 'to be transformed' is rooted in the tradition of inclusiveness, which is not only to care for the stranger but also to receive what she has to say, listen to her experience and learn different hopes, different dreams, and sing different songs.

However, I remained puzzled by the Gospel reading. John's Easter story was familiar, perhaps too well known. It is a mysterious, haunting story so different from St Paul's exhortatory style in Romans 12. I could not see how all three texts related to each other.

But then I saw a connection: the measure of an inclusive community was the extent to which forgiveness was a defining activity; as the Gospel puts it directly – 'Receive the Holy Spirit. If you forgive the sins of any they are forgiven them.' Then, and only then, to return to St Paul, its members would

> Bless those who persecute you.
> Bless and do not curse them.
> Rejoice with those who rejoice:
> Weep with those who weep.

Today the mandate to vengeance, exclusion and the making of scapegoats are all too real. The Bible issues a mighty protest and a powerful alternative: there is the hard work of building a society where all are valued; and these endeavours, as the texts reminded me, are set in the midst of God's work, who intends that all displaced persons – redundant, surplus, disposable persons – are brought into their place in the community.

How telling the sermon was I cannot say. It was after all only a tiny part in an unusual and unique celebration, but I know that at least and at last I have begun to see what the Bible can be – not as a book of rules or instructions but as a primary source for feeding the imagination towards a new, different and transformed world.

NOTES

1 From Robert Lowell, 'Waking early Sunday morning' in *Robert Lowell's Poems: A Selection*, ed. Jonathan Raban (London: Faber and Faber, 1974), p. 101.
2 E. P. Sanders and M. Davies, *Studying the Synoptic Gospels* (London: SCM Press, 1989), p. 343.
3 Luke 4.6–21.

CHAPTER

8

Men – and women

CARTER HEYWARD, an Anglican priest and teacher at the Episcopal Theological Seminary in Cambridge, Massachusetts, was the preacher for Holy Week and Easter at St James's, Piccadilly in 1990. I invited her because I knew of her writings and her reputation as a teacher. I had heard of her clarity and passion, and I was in sympathy with many of the radical causes she supported. She was among the first women to be ordained in the Anglican Church, one of the 'Philadelphia Eleven' whose ordination in 1976 was regarded as invalid if not illegal, because the General Synod of the Episcopal Church had not then agreed to ordain women. I also invited her because I hoped that many women in Britain would be encouraged by her visit to London. Women were not to be ordained priest until 1994. Then, in 1989, the possibility of women priests seemed very distant. I hoped Carter Heyward would invigorate men and women alike. She did.

Large audiences and congregations, mostly women, attended her meetings and liturgies. Carter was accompanied by her partner, Beverly Harrison – one of the most distinguished American writers on social ethics. They did a number of dialogues together, including one – not particularly appropriate for Holy Week(!) – on misogyny and homophobia, and identified the 'hatred' some men had for the 'feminine'. On Easter Day, Carter Heyward preached. She told me, just before the celebration, that she would not receive Communion in solidarity with her sisters in the Church of England who were not able to celebrate the Eucharist. She said that she would go to another part of the church, and would be prepared to give a blessing to those who felt the same as she. She was kept busy. Some 200 people gathered round her; few of those received Communion.

Her visit was invigorating, as I hoped it might be, for many women. Carter Heyward and Beverly Harrison's frankness about their sexuality – they are a lesbian couple – was eye-opening and unnerving. How could this woman with such radical views and a lesbian well and truly 'out' yet be a priest and teacher at a theological seminary?

I attended all the meetings when either or both spoke. By Easter Day I was exhausted. The exhaustion continued for some days afterwards. I could not handle the ruthless and formidable analysis and logic of feminist theology and thinking; and I found the indifference of many of the women to me personally hard. No one was directly hostile, but after a nod in my direction as the host, or as politeness demanded, I was then effectively ignored or discounted. I felt castrated, unmanned. Who was I? This was a recurring question. For many years I had supported those women who wished to be ordained priest. I had been to meetings, taken part in demonstrations, and there was I, now, experiencing something of that fear and distrust of women which I recognized in some who opposed their ordination. Alongside the fear, I felt irritated and angry that there had been no proper consultation about Easter Day. I thought then, and still do, that even on such an issue as the Ordination of Women, the celebration of Easter should have overridden all considerations. Where, I wondered, do men, do I, fit in – amongst the solidarity of these women? They could, I felt in wilder moments, destroy me altogether.

I experienced over those days a dying which is still going on: it is not comfortable to feel obliterated as a person. I was reminded of an incident at school many years ago when one of the house prefects called me up at the end of term to his study for some misdemeanour and told me 'Reeves, you've been here twelve weeks and no one noticed you'. Carter Heyward might have had some premonition of my state of mind. On Easter Day I felt there should be a sort of sign of solidarity with the women, so that everyone could, in some way, be together. Then, when the distribution of the bread and wine was completed, and when the women round Carter Heyward dispersed, I walked across to her, knelt in front of her and asked her for her blessing: she prayed that out of the empty tomb of my life new life would grow, and she extended her blessing to include the Church, all humanity and creation.

Some weeks after that Easter I spoke about these experiences to a wise woman. She reminded me that most of those who had come to hear Carter Heyward were highly articulate about patriarchy. They knew what it was to live in a culture and society where women had been for centuries defined in relation to men. They knew how for 2,500 years empires, nation states, and the modern corporate state had been dominated by men with women in a place of subordination. They knew how long women had been silenced. Now, my friend went on, we are committed to behave as women as autonomous persons valued for our gifts, and able to speak for ourselves. We refuse to be silent. Christianity, with rare exception, has mirrored this controlling, dominating, hierarchical use of power. Imagine, she said, what it would be like for you as a man in a predominantly male congregation. As a Christian you will have heard only women's voices celebrate the sacraments and preach. Only feminine words are used for yourself and others. Whenever the woman priest says 'womankind' she means all humanity. God is Mother; and in the fellowship of the congregation you experience the sisterhood of women. Your son is baptized, and he is reborn as God's daughter. You will be told that God is beyond all sexual images, but her Daughter was sent into the world to reveal God to us, and that God is fully revealed in Her. This Daughter called God Mother; we are to do the same. Only women have been chosen to represent God's authority, and the Scriptures and the tradition of the Church teach that this is so. Since in Eve all women sinned, so through her Daughter all God's daughters will be redeemed. Thus women baptize men into a new relationship with God the Mother in the power of Her spirit, where they are made daughters of God.

Some such rerun of parts of the Christian tradition is enough to show how women have been silenced by it. What is amazing is the love and loyalty which women have for the Church in spite of the way they are ridiculed as 'shrill', 'hysterical' or 'strident'; and since the ordination of women, the ferocity of attacks has not gone away. Paganism, priestesses and witchcraft: such accusations and abuse betray that fear of the irrational, uncontrollable which men perceive in women, and which I experienced briefly that Easter at St James's, Piccadilly.

After a while my exhaustion disappeared. I had, I thought, gained a little more understanding while leaving my soul more or less intact. But then at the time of the debate about the Ordination of Women, my memories of that Easter returned. The General Synod debate was hailed as a model of restraint and courtesy, an example to the rowdy immaturity of the House of Commons. I wished there had been more rowdiness. I felt much was being left unsaid, but I could not then say what that was. In the months that followed the Synod's decision, the bishops urged the Church again and again to remember the pain of those who opposed the priesthood of women. So after years and many lifetimes, women were still being victims. They could not even celebrate at the removal of this injustice: many of the gatherings leading up to the first ordination of women in Bristol Cathedral were muted and restrained. It was only then and at some other ordinations that tears of relief and liberation were shed by women and men.

I have written personally about this matter, because it is now quite clear to me that the issue of women and men in the Church has not been resolved; it has hardly begun. The novelty of a woman presiding at the Eucharist will soon disappear. All organizations seem to have a capacity and a resilience for incorporating and including change once debate and consultation have taken place.

The missing element in the movement for women's ordination has been any sense that men have to change. Bishops and priests for centuries have defined what the Church is and the place of women in the Church. We have been accustomed to ministering to women, and latterly with women; we are not used to receiving from women. We will never be able to do this, never able to willingly share our power as bishops or priests until we – the men – undergo a difficult, lengthy and painful process of repentance; repentance for our patriarchal and hierarchical structures and attitudes which we share and perpetuate and from which in terms of our livelihood we derive our security. Such repentance will be experienced as a loss – a loss of identity, a loss of power and influence. It will entail a process of dying and discovering what it means to be a man, a priest or bishop in a church and world, where men and women are working together in partnership.

*   *   *

One of the difficulties of this desire to shift fundamental assumptions and attitudes to women is that there is no consensus as to what a man is, and there is little help from Christianity, which assumes patriarchy as the norm.[1] Men are not used to describing themselves.

However, there is a debate under way about men taking place outside the churches. It is not clear where this will lead, or even if it will be successful; there are no made-to-measure, eye-catching development plans waiting to be implemented which will constitute the New Man. There is a contemporary ideal of man – Marlboro Man. He is independent, proud, self-controlled, competitive, tough, aggressive, narcissistic about his body, confused about women, contemptuous and abusive, as well as full of desire. The cost of machismo is emotional distance – from children, from women and from other men. Men, of course, talk with each other, but invariably at a distance. They also distance themselves from religion; in Roman Catholic cultures the men gather either outside or at the back of the church while the women get on with the praying led by a celibate man. Such men who aspire to this ideal never surrender, find it almost impossible to face failure; they become prisoners of perfection. I have known such men who have little sense of the sacred, even less any sense of what it is that moves them, what they long for, or what may weigh so heavily on them. These men, so used to leading, not following, acting, not receiving, controlling, not letting go, competing and not collaborating, are profoundly lonely – as soon as anything challenges their persona. Their inability to connect with either men or women (although, of course, they may be married and have a family) makes healing or growing impossible. These men, and there are many in powerful and influential positions in society, are the inevitable product of a greedy and addictive culture.

Another man is neither rich nor successful. He is the young criminal. Men are responsible for 90 per cent of indictable offences. Sixty young men are incarcerated for every one young woman. Angela Phillips, in *The Trouble With Boys*, asks 'Why does nobody ever ask why it is that so few young women, living in exactly the same unemployment, the same bad housing and cared for by the same lone mother as their male peers, end up in prison?'[2] The answer is due to the fathers who have either left or are virtually invisible as they close the door to go to work. Little boys have no models of a man to emulate as they grow up, except that of Batman and Superman, and negatively that whatever else happens little boys will not be like their mothers or their sisters. Little boys try to be like their mothers and are told not be like that. They try crying, want to go home, and they are told that boys cannot behave like that.

Men at the top, or on their way to the top, use their acquired toughness to stay there. Men at the bottom use that same toughness to become streetwise, self-sufficient, and to avoid being caught. Religion does not impinge on these men, for their whole inner life has been screened out. Wealthy, successful men, confronted with a clerical collar, either patronize out of embarrassment or revert to talking about going to school chapel at their public school. For them religion is about nostalgia if it is about anything at all. I have found that one of the most daunting parts of my job is remaining centred and being content to be foolish in the company of these men.

The writer Robert Bly believes that much of the difficulty men have in their relationships is their lack of bonding with their fathers and with other men. His writings are particularly popular with yet another sort of man – the gentle, quiet and sensitive man who has learnt to sympathize and empathize with strong women. (Some women, I am told, say to such men 'If you are gentle I will sleep with you'.) Robert Bly aims to put men in touch with their 'wild man' or 'warrior' qualities. But however these are understood, he is working in a tradition which will not easily have the blood wiped from it. There is something decidedly threatening about it, and many of the attempts at male consciousness-raising sound a little too much like the old 'white power' backlash responding to the Civil Rights movement.

I feel uneasy about these contemporary stereotypes of what a man is. I do not fit easily into any of them. But I certainly recognize the pattern of the absent father. As my mother lay dying of a malignant brain tumour, and he and I were gathered round her bed, he said to me 'We must get to know each other'. I was 35, and my father was 70. Even as he said those words I felt a deep rage against him. After the funeral, I stayed at home for some days with him, the first time we had even been alone together. It was a desultory time; and I could not leave quickly enough. My father was a naturally reticent person, whose emotional response was expressed in a wry sense of humour. But we were unable to talk to each other. My anger with him subsided; in its place I felt as if I was to blame for being such an unlovable person – what had I done wrong to deserve not being loved by my father? Over the years I have found 'father' figures, but they were not the same. Like others who have experienced this lack of primary bonding. I have done my best (and in fact, became rather adept) at concealing my disappointment, guilt and grief.

I had little idea of what I was supposed to grow up into, and as a small boy I developed a sophisticated, imaginary world into which I easily slipped. At Sherborne, and my preparatory school before that, various models as to what a man should be presented themselves, and I took to them with varying degrees of success. But I have always been conscious of an isolation, incompleteness and lack of connection with others which has affected my close relationships with men and women.

My absent father has made it more or less impossible for me to conceive God as Father – the primary, traditional and controlling image of God in Christianity. I have come to prefer those images of God which speak of God's closeness and immanence – as mother, or friend, lover, or brother.

My experience is not unusual and is echoed in much of the discussions about men. And all this is a long way from the pronouncements, admonitions, and advice about relationships and sexuality which emerge from time to time from the churches.

As I write, homosexuality is the subject which is before the public eye. All the mainline denominations take variations of 'Go and see what they are doing and tell them to stop it', or 'Go and see what they are doing, or want to do, and tell them they can't', or 'Go and see what they are doing and say the boys can but the prefects can't because they have to set an example'. What church leaders fail to realize is that the vast majority of Christian people take little notice of these pronouncements as guides to living; our behaviour is governed not by deference to authority, but by a whole range of other factors.

For many years on Sunday evenings on LBC local radio I was a clerical agony uncle on a phone-in. For one-and-a-half hours I remember conversations about rape, incest, abuse, compulsive, neurotic or addictive sexual behaviour. I recall conversations about the break-up of marriages and partnerships, and the physical violence which so often went with them. Many calls were about people's loneliness, and how so many lives seemed unlived. There were conversations about jealousy and the fear of rejection. There were calls from the victims of racism and homophobia, and from young gay people asking whether or not they should 'come out' to their parents. I remember conversations with exhausted carers of elderly relatives and with young people caring for their friends and lovers dying of AIDS.

Not once was there a question about the teaching of Christianity on sexual matters; and in a much more limited way, as a pastor, my conversations have always been about relationships, about helping men and women to make the very best of them. I have never been concerned to make people 'obey' the rules set down by ecclesiastical authorities. The rules, and the arguments, do not tally or make sense faced with the muddle, complexities, agonies and delight of experience. And I am not advocating anarchy or unbridled hedonism – far from it: there is evident longing for relationships – partnerships, marriages, and families (of different sorts) – to work out, in the interests of themselves, their children and their neighbours.

Christianity has little to contribute to our understanding of sexuality and relationships, as long as its statements by bishops and others are reduced to ethics – 'You should or should not do this.' Christianity also contributes little directly to the sort of counselling I did publicly on the phone-in programmes or privately. What is missing between the giving of advice on the one hand and listening hard on the other is a more positive evaluation of sexuality, desire and intimacy as paths to holiness and to God. When sexuality is mentioned it is swept under the carpet, as an activity, different and separate. That is the real scandal of the Church's attitude to sex.

However, the rejection of patriarchy provides the chance of learning to integrate sexuality into the rest of our experience, although there is a difficulty in finding the appropriate language to write about these matters. To speak more positively about sexuality begins to sound like D. H. Lawrence or Bhagwan Rajneesh. Our over-lyrical expressions of what is only too often grubby, messy and unsatisfactory is as useless as the flat language of ecclesiastics: same-sex relationships are treasured and honoured, as long as they are 'non-genital'.

Nevertheless, I sense a need, particularly among younger people, to be less superficial about sex. There are two areas which need exploring and debating. One is desire, and the other is intimacy. Desire is usually understood as being entirely mindless and irrational; it just happens. But that is not so; a person may be aroused sexually by what he or she sees, but he or she will have choices to make. It is not always necessary to follow that object of desire! It is possible to learn what we need and desire. That is a self-knowledge which deepens as part of the inner life of the spirit, which I described in Chapter 4. It is possible to become aware of desire, which is less than mere gratification or release, and more in the direction of a regard, or affection for another. And if poets like John Donne or mystics like St Teresa of Avila or St John of the Cross are to be trusted, then that love may be a sign of the love of God which, unlike all our attempts at loving, is utterly faithful and constant.

The befriending of our desire is the essential moral core of sexuality. When it is said of someone that he is still sexually active at 70 or 80 that sounds like an old engine kept in good condition. It is a mechanical image, and as such adds to the reductionist views on sexuality. But a sign of the sexually mature person, whether man or woman, is to learn what he or she desires and acts or not, as the occasion demands. In phone-in programmes that I have taken part in more recently I have tried to help callers think about their desires and to differentiate between them.

The other aspect of sexuality which needs affirming is that which applies to those in a sexual relationship, but also to everyone else – single, celibate, elderly, as well as young – that is, the degree to which we are able to be intimate with one another. By intimacy, I mean the extent to which men or women are prepared to be tender, compassionate and close, even touching one another, and across all boundaries. Heterosexual men find this intimacy particularly troubling. (Some dislike the practice of hugging one another at the Peace in the Eucharist.) There are fears of being considered too feminine, too soft, or of discovering that they are gay. That is why men's groups are one of the ways in which bonding with other men can happen, and such a freedom assists in their relations with everyone else, including women.

One of the oddest bits of evidence that I can bring forward for the way in which sexuality is so troubling and difficult, is behaviour at weddings. Since I have been ordained I have celebrated about 1,500 wedding ceremonies. I have wondered why they are so often uneasy, anxious and distracted occasions. I used to think that it was the strangeness of the setting – church buildings which most of the congregation had not visited. But I have learnt from listening to people that weddings evoke a variety of emotions. There is, of course, a concern and hope for the couple being married. But there is also often a regret of those whose marriages have not worked out. There are the single people, sometimes elderly, who have never known what it is to be loved by another. There are single people – perhaps close friends of the bride or bridegroom – who will begin to feel excluded. There are gay or lesbian people whose own partnerships cannot be acknowledged or blessed by the Church. There are those who are uncertain as to whether they should commit themselves to the same road as their friends who are married. Wedding receptions can be quite melancholy celebrations. This is because there is so little understanding about the riches of sexuality or the nature of friendship with its many steps of intimacy. And because there is a lack of appreciation about the possible riches of sexuality, the befriending of desire and perhaps the celebration of friendship, with the many steps of intimacy involved, people experience anxiety and a sense of loss and isolation.

*   *   *

There is little in the Bible or 2,000 years of Christian experience to help men move away from the closed system of patriarchy. Together with other men, and together with women, there is a need to address honestly and carefully some of the matters which I have touched on, recognizing always that the narratives of our lives are the material out of which our moral concerns are educated and formulated.

My concern in writing about myself as a man with an ingrained patriarchal mind-set, yet wanting to break out of it, is to find ways in which I and other men will discover what real partnership between men and women could become.

One of the points in which connections are made is when tears come. Tears can be an epiphany, when, as the eyes fill, they reveal more than we might think. Tears are often a cement in a relationship; they seal a common bond between us, and give the lie to the notion of individualism. We are connected whether we like it or not.

Tears seem to be such a private matter. We cry, and we do not know why, at a piece of music, at the sight of a landscape, a child asleep. They well up unexpectedly, sometimes endlessly. They can be signs of anger; or signs of the tenderest love. Tears reveal the values we live by and share with one another. Tears are the unexplored connections between us all of whatever gender, age or race. They are a bridge between us all, flimsy as it is. But there is something invigorating about thinking that the bridge over troubled waters is really made up of the water itself.

Our tears, which men and women can shed together, are signs of God's passion – our God-given capacity to feel, to endure, to empathize with, to live fully and well. It is, as Simone Weil described it, 'living with attention'.

*   *   *

This brief excursion into some of the issues around being a man and sexuality are necessary in a chapter entitled 'Men – and women', because sooner or later men will necessarily have to join women in what is called – in the ugliest of words – eco-feminism.

Eco-feminism is the merging of those passionate about the environment, and those women who are refusing to be silent. The year 1963 saw the publication of three books whose impact is still with us over thirty years on. One was John Robinson's *Honest to God*; another was Rachel Carson's *Silent Spring*; and the other was Betty Friedan's *The Feminine Mystique*. *Honest to God* was an exploration into the reality of God at the point of our deepest concerns; John Robinson shifted the image of God from a transcendent father figure in the sky to the knowledge of 'the Other' revealed through relationships. He did not write about either environmentalism or feminism, but in bringing God 'down to earth' prepared the ground, quite unintentionally, for much of the discussion about God in both these movements. The two women writers, Rachel Carson and Betty Friedan, released new ideas which have developed into two movements, growing rapidly and now beginning to merge. *Silent Spring* was one of the seeds of the environmental movement. It crystallized an already existing discussion on disintegration and slow destruction of the environment in the USA. *The Feminine Mystique* crystallized another discussion – a straightforward attack on the stereotyping which kept middle-class women locked away in suburbia, cut off from educational and employment opportunities that would allow them to compete for jobs.

Both books were the beginning of developing movements. From a growing awareness of the destruction of the environment developed a powerful environmental movement – even if it has yet to be acknowledged in public policies. Then developed a concern for nature for its own sake, and a realization that it deserved to be treated with respect. Now there is a sense that all life on earth is interconnected and interdependent.

The Feminine Mystique launched, at least in the public eye, the feminist movement where women organized themselves to liberate themselves from male domination and struggled to shed their second-class status. This developed into insights about the deeply embodied nature of patriarchy, not just in contemporary society but throughout the birth of civilization and the growth of urban cultures. Embracing the situation of women throughout the world, feminism has developed into a fundamental criticism of culture.

Both movements are egalitarian. Women refuse to be silent as men tell them 'what is right or good' for them.

'We' are not, of course, just women, but men, women and children together; new forms of community will begin to happen. The churches are already communities – of a sort. As men and women are slowly able to step aside from the aggressive, machismo and addictive world, so Christians and other communities of resistance and celebration will emerge. They will be signs of our committed love for one another, for the earth and for God.

NOTES

1 But see *Theology and Sexuality* (the journal of the Institute for the Study of Christianity and Sexuality: March 1995), particularly James B. Nelson, 'On doing Body theology', p. 38.
2 Angela Phillips, *The Trouble With Boys* (Pandora Press, 1993).

9

Community[1]

I HAVE BEEN WRITING about the ways in which those of us who are believers, or are in the way to being believers, or would like to be, can contribute to the healing of the planet, which requires us to both think and act locally and globally.

I write from the experience of a particular constituency – the Church of England – which I love and which I have served for thirty years, although not without exasperation and impatience. I cannot now remember a time when we were so unsure as to what or who we are; we lack self-confidence, and are becoming more self-engrossed, self-absorbed and self-centred. There is nothing like a financial crisis to provoke introspection. We are in no position, as we are, to undertake the steps I have proposed – without a massive trust in the imagination, and the capacity to let go of so much that seems necessary for our security and future.

I have listened to the experiences of many who have found themselves drawn to Christianity, and to their local church – either for the first time or after a prolonged period of absence. What I have found is an almost unanimous disillusionment with the way churches are organized and carry out their business.

The Church is perceived by the newcomer as inviting a lot of her energy and time. This is what is called in a deadening phrase 'lay participation' – not just in the liturgy but in committees and small groups. These are the sub-committees of churches, and the more flourishing the church, the more committees. It is rare to find much excitement about these activities. While there are a few whose lives are driven by meetings, and some who feel it is a reasonable and necessary part of membership, the reasons are usually less exalted: to 'help out the Vicar', or because there is no one else, or because it has become a habit, or as an excuse to get away from their families, or from a sense of guilt. There is not usually much that is enjoyable or liberating about 'stewardship', 'finance', 'building' committees. It is not necessary to labour the point, but enthusiasm soon gives way to disillusionment. What is the point of these activities except to maintain the institution as it is? Meanwhile, as elderly people die and there are fewer younger people to replace them, the 'system' will become less and less manageable.

Of course, this pedestrian and negative aspect of 'church life' is one-sided: it does not include what are its more redeeming features – lively worship, successful projects; and it takes no account of the many private acts of kindness and care which should occur naturally in every Christian community. But it is obvious that as the Church conducts its affairs locally, it is quite unable to address the ecological and environmental madness which is the context of this book. And it should be said that the central organizations of the Church, which in theory exist primarily to service the local church, do nothing of the sort; they appear to exist for their own survival. I was not only a member of the General Synod, but also an *ex officio* member of the Diocesan Synod, and Area Synod. I am a member of the Deanery Synod, the Chapter of local clergy, and chairperson of the Parochial Church Council. Each of these groups has a committee structure which becomes more sophisticated and more busy with the attendant bureaucracy, paper work, and plethora of meetings, the nearer you get to the General Synod.

There have to be other ways of 'being Church', whose members can break free from their unwitting apostasy, respond to the lure of God and take their places among those who struggle for the healing of the planet. The solution does not lie, primarily, in re-organizing the structures of the institution. Reorganization is already under way, determined in the case of the Church of England by its considerable financial restrictions, and in the Roman Catholic Church by its acute shortage of priests. What will emerge, and are already doing, are leaner and slimmer churches.

I am not sure that there are solutions or answers, but I am clear about the approach. This is, as I have said in Chapter 4, to trust the experience of the people, to acknowledge and to guard the confusion and chaos which times of change always bring. There are two other considerations – one is the need for a continual struggle through the fog of our addictions, denial and despair which I have already noted, and to wake up to the state of the planet. We are so tied into present systems of consumption that we can barely imagine alternatives that might bring greater peace and more permanent security, even though the effort to 'keep up' leaves us all more insecure, anxious and exhausted. The change of consciousness I have been advocating is an ongoing process, a lifetime's work. It will not happen in a movement, or through grand gestures of self-sacrifice. Such changes will be painful, messy, and cannot be made individually: we need one another.

The second consideration is the attempt to integrate and to make connections between the life of faith and everything else. I have tried, in different periods of my ministry, to spend time in people's work places to help them and myself make connections between their work and what is said and done on Sundays. Rarely have I been able to contribute anything useful: the gap between life and worship is (in spite of all the talking and writing) quite enormous. Bits of our lives are separated; we inhabit many different worlds. The ecological crisis compels us to integrate our lives, to strive after a 'wholeness' which brings together business and commercial lives, the personal and domestic lives, the political and economic, the local, regional, national and international.

This need for a more holistic approach presents itself from another perspective. I have been to many a meeting which, as the agenda is worked through, provokes questions about the fundamental purpose of our activities. Sometimes there have been strong, personal testimonies; sometimes an awareness of the gap between what we say and do; sometimes a desire to stay together, to struggle with the requirements and demands of faith so that there is a more vibrant, joyful and true witness. The conversation begins to be inescapable, but then everyone gets up, goes home, until the next meeting. The rest of life has to go on, but what if it was possible, and felt desirable, that such a congregation or group were in closer contact, closer relationship, one with another, what would such a community look like?

From the outside it might appear to be some sort of commune: a congregation comes into being which consists of different sorts of households. Some will share their accommodation; others their skills; others their financial resources. Some will join a community such as this for a period, and then return to a more conventional way of living; others will live as they always have done but actively support and encourage those who have begun to live more closely with one another. A crucial test of the way these communities function is the manner in which financial matters are handled. Some who are in work may gladly support those who are unemployed and who are indispensable to the life of the community. For example, artists of one sort or another are necessary for developing rituals and liturgies. In such a congregation both hierarchy and patriarchy can be questioned, and the ordained minister will not necessarily be the leader, or the sole leader.

There is an 'alternative' feel to what I am describing: yet there is little that is new or original. Christianity has a wealth of experience of those who are called to live 'in community'; and no doubt one of the possibilities which might be considered is some sort of religious order, in which vows are taken, perhaps on a temporary basis. Communal living in whatever form often arises at critical times either in the Church or in the world. We are at such a point now.

The sustaining and nurture of the households I have described will be a variety of rituals, liturgies and therapies, some of which I have already outlined. The middle classes are always in danger of fitful idealism, chasing one good cause after another, and the steadiness and steadfastness of purpose will only be maintained by a hidden discipline. And yet discipline is not quite the right word, for what is required is time to let go of fears, to open up to each other and to the world around us. The struggle to challenge and to change the values and assumptions of our wearisome addictions to materialism has to be rooted in the grace of God, in the goodness of life; it means to be in touch with the living earth, and it means to release our intuitive, creative and imaginative powers. We will also need to shape together liturgies which begin to reflect our altered consciousness, so that we can mourn together for the way in which life (and the earth) have been violated, bring to birth healing and taste a new creation already present. I have visited some communities where there is so much emphasis on struggle, and an overwhelming absence of grace, that I could not leave quickly enough. On the other hand, contrary to the solemnity of much institutional religion, I have experienced some of the best parties after a demonstration among marginalized groups. As it used to be said in the 1960s, 'unless there's dancing at the Revolution I'm not coming!'

There is nothing particularly virtuous in advocating alternative households within and on the edge of Christian congregations. There is certainly nothing easy about living so closely with others, whom one may not naturally like but to whom we are drawn because of sharing similar truths. The call to move into exile, to experience a new freedom and vitality there to respond to the God who is luring us back into life to help heal our planet.

The process of establishing communities is painful; it means learning how to deal not only with money but with power and sex – all matters which give rise to disagreement and conflict, and which could destroy and have destroyed them. Christianity is scarred with the failure of community living: there are the ancient religious orders living closely to the ideals of a Benedict, Dominic or Francis: and as these institutions sometimes grow away from their founder's intentions either they have to be renewed or they die out. Then there are tiny households and communities sharing a simple and similar lifestyle, but sometimes even here the struggle for power brings pain and destruction in its wake.

There is one criterion for establishing the size of these congregations, communities and households, and that is that every member has to be valued. One of the problems of so many congregations of, say, 50 or 70 people is that for a newcomer it can be too much of a crowd. There is, of course, no guarantee that a smaller 'unit' is any more welcoming. But within any gathering of over 30 people there need to be opportunities for inter-action in a more intimate way, so that the gifts of everyone concerned do not lie dormant or unappreciated, but can be developed and celebrated.

As I said in Chapter 4, discussing the role and function of bishops, the fragmentation of the Church into tiny households and groups is not enough. The networking of smaller units as part of a larger whole is necessary – for without networking, the tyranny of the small, enclosed group can take over and have little or nothing to contribute to the purpose beyond the life of the group itself.

How is it possible to handle failure in a society and church where 'success' is a significant criterion for living? One answer to this has been offered by one who knows about the difficulties and opportunities the communal life affords. Thomas Cullinan lives on the edge of Liverpool. Eleven years ago four monks set off to build a monastery: one died. Another fell in love and left; another became a convent chaplain. He was alone, and has remained alone ever since, although he is supported by friends and visitors who work and pray with him, and he has remained within the Benedictine tradition as it is expressed in Ampleforth, which is his 'family' for life. The Benedictine life is not to do good works but to establish a 'school of the Lord's service', where monks would learn to discover God in everyday life: that is the rationale behind the pattern of work, prayer and silence.

Thomas Cullinan writes eloquently about injustice, about the growing gap between rich and poor, and about the call to be in solidarity with the poorest of the poor. He knows about the despair which suffocates the ability to change. And he writes:

> The heart of the Christian message is that the most salvific moment in the history of the world was when one man was pinned to a cross unable to do anything for anybody about anything. Until we can come to the point of living in presence of unbearable inability to do anything, I don't think we've really entered into the presence of a crucified God.[2]

To most ears, that sounds complete nonsense. After all, what is so special about powerlessness, about a state of being where we can no longer order ourselves or others about?

It is easy to recognize the opposite state – when an individual or a community begins to say: 'Isn't God lucky to have us? Are we not the chosen ones, doing good in the name of Christ?'

Some years ago I was rung up by the chaplain of Wandsworth prison: would we be able to take in a young man just finishing a short sentence for theft? 'Of course', we said, 'Anything to help.' John arrived, captivated everyone, and soon became part of the inner circle of the church, making himself indispensable. Our haloes began to shine: 'Look', we were saying, 'how good and caring we have been.' One day, £400 was missing from the safe. John disappeared. A few days later he appeared, quite penitent. After a long conversation with me he was restored to the community. Once again we became pleased with ourselves: we had shown ourselves to be a caring community yet again, and this time we had accepted and received one who had stolen from us. Some weeks later, £500 was found missing from the safe. John disappeared. Neither he nor the money has ever been found.

To acknowledge powerlessness is to be more considered, thoughtful, and realistic. In John's case it would have meant recognizing that John was a recidivist and had many convictions. We should have known we could have done very little, perhaps at the most contain him. We paid for our superiority, arrogance and blindness to John's situation. We were more concerned with our own conscience than with John's wellbeing.

In facing up to the madness of environmental destruction, the powerlessness and sense of despair, as we have noted, is only too familiar. Yet powerlessness is not hopelessness. It recognizes with due humility the fragility and transience of men and women. We exist for a season. Our bodies shrivel, the structures that sustain our lives fail, and we die. Our bodies, alongside those of animals, birds, reptiles, insects, trees and plants, disintegrate into organic matter, and enter a cycle of decomposition and recomposition. We come out of the earth; we return to the earth – whoever we are. Like the earthling formed out of the living soil in Genesis, we recall that 'Dust thou art, and into dust thou shalt return'. Our bodies – the flesh and blood of which they are composed – live on in plants and animals and all living things; our bodies are themselves composed of substances that are parts of everything else stretching back to the formation of the earth, and the dust of exploding stars. The transience of ourselves is not the tragic aloneness of the human soul, but an awareness of our kinship, our bond with the earth.

What I am describing is neither romantic nor a maudlin fantasy. It is simply the way everything is, and the way everything is in its interdependence. And it leads to compassion, to suffering with, rejoicing with; and the compassion, as it is generated, releases energy and passion for justice and for the healing of the planet. That is how our powerlessness changes in the light of our growing awareness of our interdependence, all part of the web of living.

What will distinguish the corporate life of these new communities is modesty and humility. Who will belong to these communities, and what will they do?

Those who belong believe that what now exists cannot be all there is. They do not give in to the pervading, mild cynicism which forbids the dream of a different world or ridicules it. There is a sense of recognition that, as the Quakers put it, there is that of God in every person, which means simply that faith in God and in one another, love for God and for one another, and hope towards God and towards one another, cannot be extinguished.

The difficulties of mobilizing the imagination in this direction cannot be underestimated in a society which is so captivated by nostalgia and to the recreating of a past of small market towns, cathedral cities, village greens, cricket, costume drama on television and Merchant–Ivory films in the cinema. Anything which disturbs this vision of the past (as in some way exemplary for today) like motorways, council estates or ethnic minorities has been deliberately erased.

Christianity's vigorous utopian tradition pushes the boundaries of the present out, and responds to God's passion for justice, the divine manifestation of the love of God. There is a recklessness, impatience, about this: as the Bible says, 'Seek ye first the Kingdom of God, and all the rest shall be added unto you'.

The membership of these communities will grow out of existing congregations among its loyal members as well as those on the edge – the disappointed and disaffected ones; and I am not writing for the Church of England alone. With the ecumenical movement stuck, many are losing patience with traditional denominational differences; and are beginning to pick and choose the community to which they will attach themselves.

The question of the task of such communities has already been largely answered. The 'inner work', the arduous work of creating ritual and liturgy, the developing of the imagination in relation to both the Bible and the Christian tradition, the offering of hospitality and the celebrating of the public – these are the basis of the renewed communities.

But as the awareness of the ecological crisis begins to permeate, so priorities will change. In the 1960s, the World Council of Churches produced a slogan: 'Let the world set the agenda.' This meant that the Church's ministry was to be defined by the needs of the world, wherever and whatever they were; Christ was a servant to all, and Christians were to follow that example of service.

However, this slogan and the activities with which it was associated soon disappeared. Many conservative and traditionalist Christians said that the Church's agenda was not to be set by the world because it led to the easiest sort of liberalism where secular trends would determine the nature and character of faith – hence some objections to the ordination of women have been expressed as merely endorsing fashionable views about feminism. Trendy bishops and liberal clergy have now become only too familiar scapegoats for all the misfortunes of the Church.

Yet 'Let the world set the agenda' now needs to be rehabilitated with all available urgency, imagination and passion. In *Beyond the Limits*, the authors acknowledge 'that the limits are real and close, and that there is just exactly enough time, with no time to waste. There is just exactly enough energy, enough material, enough money, enough environmental resilience and enough human virtue to bring about a revolution to a better world.'[3] Revolution begins to be a real, workable alternative to the present order. It does not just mean riding bicycles, recycling paper, bottles and tins, becoming vegetarian. It means working out appropriate 'lifestyles' – not supporting organizations which oppress people and abuse the Earth. It means restricting the number of children in families, investing appropriately, taking care of land where possible. It means being watchful of governments, creating networks and coalitions. It means repealing some laws, and adding others. It means educating children and re-educating ourselves. It means new farming methods, and new forms of business. It means rethinking the nature of work and leisure. It means drawing on the creativity and imagination of each of us, and of those who have to be artists to give us a hint of this new world. It means including, not excluding, celebrating the rich diversity of the planet; it means resisting racism, anti-Semitism and homophobia; it means challenging the arms race; it means restoring local and regional governments; it means encouraging 'subversives in place': those in government, in public service, in politics, in non-governmental organizations, trusts and foundations, who sense the need for explorations and addressing new questions. Christian communities, alongside many other communities and networks, could be the cradle for the sustainable revolution where, through public debate, alternative forums to those of government will come into being.

And when all that is happening – that is not enough. No one knows what enough is. There has to be enough wisdom and compassion to halt the limitless growth, and to look for ways for this sustainable revolution to flourish – not just for the more industrialized countries but all the inhabitants of the earth, and for the earth itself. There needs to emerge not hasty technological fixes, but a willingness to restrain, to hold back, so that healing of the planet may begin.

One element missing from these emerging communities is the Teacher of Wisdom. I am sometimes asked if I could suggest the name of a wise man or woman who might help someone troubled or confused. The question is difficult to answer – wisdom is in short supply.

As an undergraduate I occasionally visited an Anglican priest. My memories of my visits and our conversations are of someone who was absolutely attentive and respectful to whatever I had to say; he spoke a good deal of common sense about my problems, managing to put them in a broader context, thus taking some of the pressures out of them. His study was crammed with books – not just in the bookshelves but on chairs, tables and the floor, and not just theology. He was a chain smoker and his clerical shirt was always marked with cigarette ash. I associate him with books and cigarettes, and being there – for me. Such priests have now nearly disappeared from the Church of England. And if our pay and our livelihood depend on our performance at getting more 'bums on seats' then my friend would soon be out of a job.

We did not talk often about God, but when we did it was always as part of conversation where it was absolutely natural and easy to do so. I sensed someone who knew what he was talking about and also someone who was respectful of experience, whatever it was. Today I would express that in terms of one who was rooted and grounded in the Christian tradition, but who recognized the mystery and inscrutability of God; and space for this mystery was never crowded out or explained away. The mystery was honoured. My friend's presence was always reassuring. Today I would say that he had a proper ecological sense of the interconnectedness of all things, however much it was broken up and marred by wickedness. Our relationship was not that of a therapist and client, or one of academic and undergraduate, but of two people standing before the mystery and muddle of life.

A world which is on the threshold of enormous change will need to look for wisdom. But where is it to be found? Not in the universities. Here theologians are under constant pressures to keep their jobs by writing books and engaging in research. There is less and less opportunity for confessional theology (where the 'thinking' is related directly to the experience of the church), and more pressure to keep theology as an academic subject, which could as well be taught by a Muslim or an atheist. Such wisdom is not found in bishops or the clergy; they have neither the time nor the inclination; it is not nurtured in theological colleges where too much has to be digested too quickly. Not in cathedrals where the staff are required to be proficient in finances and administration above almost everything else.[4]

There is a place today for the Teacher of Wisdom. Churches do not by right, or by their nature, have the resources for this work. It cannot be assumed that wisdom will just be available. Yet without it, organized religion is open to bigotry, superstition and fanaticism.

But the alternative communities that I have sketched should become homes for such women and men as the need for such persons is expressed. If, for example, there are concerns for closer forms of community then it would be only natural to have among them one who has absorbed the insights and experience of, say, the Benedictine way. The experience of the past will throw light on the way a community is formed in the present and for the future. If there are women whose training, skills and experience are in theology, the environment and feminism, then they will readily find a home (not least because some universities will not employ them). If churches begin to share their financial resources for those who help to create rituals and liturgies, then there has to be a place on the same basis for Teachers of Wisdom.

Such teachers will invariably be elderly – at least over 50, for they will have weathered and reflected on experience; wisdom entails brooding and thoughtfulness. There is a fashion to teach people in their thirties to be spiritual directors. There may be some who have the gifts of discernment, but wisdom needs experience – refracted, reflected on, and interpreted. When Dorothee Sölle came to St James's, Piccadilly, I introduced her as a radical biblical thinker, feminist and liberation theologian. I said she was married with three children. Before Dorothee began her address, she gently and publicly admonished me, saying that I had omitted something important from my introduction – that she was a grandmother. The collective power of grandmothers and grandfathers who have absorbed their life's experience and their own religious traditions has yet to be realized!

NOTES

1 I would like to acknowledge the help I received from Rosemary Radford Ruether, *Gaia and God* (London: SCM Press, 1993), particularly chapter 10.
2 Judith Rice, *New Testaments* (London: Fount, 1993), p. 251.
3 Donella H. Meadows, Dennis L. Meadows and Jorgen Randers, *Beyond the Limits* (London; Earthscan, 1992), p. 236.

4 *Heritage and Renewal – The Report of the Archbishops' Commission on Cathedrals* (Church House Publishing, 1994). In the index there are extensive references to fabric, finance, governance, management structure and process – and only one reference to cathedral programmes of theological education!

Afterword

SITTING THROUGH GENERAL SYNOD DEBATES, I have wondered more than once whether I am not just writing for myself in view of the fact that the present concerns of the Church of England, or of any other denominations, are hardly reflected in everything I have written.

The markers that I have put down for the future invite change on a considerable scale; none of them will happen without struggle. To propose the restoring of a vigorous public life, the developing of a variety of rituals, the bringing to birth of a new spiritual leadership, and the forming of Christian ecological households and communities – these, just to name a few, require change in attitudes, beliefs and practice.

Change begins when the imagination is mobilized. Then our capacity to perceive the world differently undermines our accommodation to old ways of thinking, believing and living.

That is why the gospel is good news; the word is derived from the Old English 'godspel', which itself is the translation of the Greek word 'evangelion' which means 'good announcement'. The news is neither whimsical nor fanciful. It is news that is neither reactionary – in which old certainties are rigidly repeated – nor news that is popular, merely reflecting what we all wish to hear. The news is good because it is radical. And in *Down to Earth* I have sketched the contours of a radical church.